Angels and Superheroes

PRAISE FOR *ANGELS AND SUPERHEROES*

"In these challenging times today we certainly need *Angels and Heroes* to keep us energized to support dynamic student learning and help young people overcome life's challenges. Whether it is called 'grit' or 'persistence,' educators need to model the positive approach that principal Jack M. Jose and intervention specialist Krista L. Taylor have taken in their writing and actions. This new book is on my 'best reading list' for teachers!"—**Rae L. White, chair, Department of Education, Muskingum University**

"In these days of high-stakes testing and accountability ratings, it's refreshing to read the words of Jack M. Jose and Krista L. Taylor. Their work reminds us that education is more than labeling and data trends—it's also taking care of our students and nurturing their dreams. Add the ideas of this book to your list of best practices. When the student comes first, learning will follow."—**Mark White, superintendent, New Albany Schools, Ohio, and coauthor of *What's in Your Space: 5 Steps for Better School and Classroom Design* and *Leading Schools in Disruptive Times***

"Few professions, if any, provide more lasting value to society than teachers. A good teacher changes lives and makes the world a better place. In *Angels and Superheroes*, Jose and Taylor provide practical advice for how to do this important but challenging work in an even more effective and meaningful way—even in circumstances that conspire against it."—**Craig Weber, author of *Conversational Capacity: The Secret to Building Teams That Perform When the Pressure Is On***

Angels and Superheroes

Compassionate Educators in an Era of School Accountability

JACK M. JOSE AND KRISTA L. TAYLOR

ROWMAN & LITTLEFIELD
Lanham • Boulder • New York • London

Published by Rowman & Littlefield
A wholly owned subsidiary of The Rowman & Littlefield Publishing Group, Inc.
4501 Forbes Boulevard, Suite 200, Lanham, Maryland 20706
www.rowman.com

Unit A, Whitacre Mews, 26-34 Stannary Street, London SE11 4AB

British Library Cataloguing in Publication Information Available

Library of Congress Cataloging-in-Publication Data

Names: Jose, Jack M., 1969- author. | Taylor, Krista L., 1970- author.
Title: Angels and superheroes : compassionate educators in an era of school accountability / Jack M. Jose and Krista L. Taylor.
Description: Lanham, Maryland : Rowman & Littlefield, [2018] | Includes bibliographical references.
Identifiers: LCCN 2017048864 (print) | LCCN 2017059472 (ebook) | ISBN 9781475838039 (electronic) | ISBN 9781475838015 (hardback : alk. paper) | ISBN 9781475838022 (pbk. : alk. paper)
Subjects: LCSH: Classroom management—United States. | Teacher-student relationships—United States. | Teachers—Professional relationships—United States. | Academic achievement—United States. | Educational accountability—United States. | Education—Standards—United States.
Classification: LCC LB3013 (ebook) | LCC LB3013 .J67 2018 (print) | DDC 371.102/4—dc23
LC record available at https://lccn.loc.gov/2017048864

∞™ The paper used in this publication meets the minimum requirements of American National Standard for Information Sciences—Permanence of Paper for Printed Library Materials, ANSI/NISO Z39.48-1992.

Printed in the United States of America

For Kathy
—J. M. J.

For Blake
—K. L. T.

Contents

Foreword

This is a wise and deeply moving book, reporting in honest and encouraging words a record of life in the highly challenging atmosphere of American high schools today. Its authors—Jack Jose, principal, and Krista Taylor, intervention specialist—are the veteran leaders of Gamble Montessori High School, a district public high school established in an impoverished area of Cincinnati, Ohio, in 2005. Their combined experience of over 30 years "in the trenches" with students, parents, and teaching colleagues gives authenticity to the hope and inspiration that shine on every page of their story.

These authors have fully grasped what is so desperately lacking in education today, with its emphasis on "teach, memorize, test, then measure." Their focus instead is based on the recognition that there is a human spirit within each one of us, young and old alike. It is this human spirit that gives us our value as individual human beings and is the basis of our potential for development through the experiences of our lives. Reaching that human spirit within each child and student is the necessary foundation of a meaningful education from elementary school onward, not academic instruction alone.

Jose and Taylor developed this focus for their own approach to education through careful observation of their students in school settings, both privileged and underserved, and through a realization that, historically, when educators place an emphasis on observation of their students and subsequent revealed needs versus abstract instruction, intellectual development exceeds expectations. Observation of phenomena and subsequent study of facts are identified as the basis of all dramatic human progress in almost every field. Yet, for some reason, in the schooling of our young, we are stuck in the last century, unable to see the boredom, lack of interest, and minimal academic success so evident for far too many students in classrooms today.

The authors have found inspiration and guidance for their teaching approach in the work of the Italian physician turned global educator Dr. Maria Montessori, who developed her educational principles through a focus on observations of children from birth to young adulthood. Jose and Taylor have applied these Montessori principles to their work with Gamble students by sensitively observing how these principles support adolescents throughout their development, and thereby have established a successful model for their school.

Perhaps the most basic of Montessori's principles, developed from her lifelong observation of children and young adults throughout the world, is the recognition that human beings develop throughout their formative years from birth to age 24 years in distinct stages and in response to their surroundings. The human spirit within each child seeks to respond in positive ways to his or her immediate environment, ways that will aid formation into a complete human being of developed intellect, controlled will, and joyful response to the world and others within it. To bring forth this positive result, however, depends most strongly upon the surrounding culture of the child, including, importantly, the adults within it.

It follows then that attention of parents and teachers must be given first and foremost to preparing a suitable environment for the young, first within the home, but next, and every bit as importantly, within the school. Just as this careful preparation is particularly important in the first years of childhood, it is equally essential in the first years of adulthood, the years from 12 to 18 years. Jose and Taylor have grasped these Montessori principles and made them the hallmarks of Gamble Montessori High School.

How the authors have managed to establish a school culture that fosters positive self-formation in their students, in spite of all the obstacles in the latters' daily lives in their homes and neighborhoods, is the story of *Angels and Superheroes*. It is told with humility and full recognition of the necessary failures and mistakes, for adults, for children, and for adolescents, inherent in the learning process. Indeed, I think it is fair to say that they regard Gamble Montessori, and their day-to-day solutions of its specific situations, as "a work in progress." Yet their hard-earned wisdom to date fills every page of their book, and their generosity in sharing lessons learned is a gift to every teacher and principal of both elementary and high schools today.

The foundation of their wisdom is the recognition that each child and young person is a unique human being, never created before nor to be created again. Each one has talents and gifts to be developed. For teachers to discover them, they have to know each student intimately and earn their trust and respect. In the words of Principal Jose, good teachers are in the business of "meeting children where they are." It is up to the leadership of the school to make this possible for teachers to do. This means creating a school culture that does not give more students to any one teacher per day than he or she can relate to on a very personal basis. It also means creating continuity of relationship between teacher and students over several or more years. The authors' strategies for managing this seemingly impossible outcome in a large public high school are carefully outlined for the reader and surprised me in their simplicity. As a result of these strategies, respect and understanding of human uniqueness are essential products of a very specific Gamble Montessori culture.

A second pillar of this culture is equally important to its success, however. It is the attention and energy given to building a sense of community. All children need to feel part of a community of others, and progressively so as they reach their high school years and begin to look to the larger world for meaning and acceptance. The way in which the authors suggest building school community initially came as a surprise to me, just as did their ability to create a culture of lasting interpersonal relationships between teacher and student. They begin with developing community among the teachers rather than community among the students. Jose and Taylor maintain that it is through the teachers modeling community among themselves that the students will be able to understand and build community and love of their school for themselves.

Of course, upon reflection, this makes perfect sense, and I realize that the schools I know that are the most outstanding have also had a mantra of building community within the teaching team first. In this way, students have an example of individuals mentoring and supporting one another, respecting each other's differences and uniting in undertaking communal responsibilities. The school principal has to be the leader of his or her team in this endeavor, providing structure and opportunities, formal and informal, for constructive community building, and the authors present excellent practical strategies for doing so. Armed with their own growth in building true community among peers, teachers are enabled to build community in their individual classroom cultures, and the advantages of doing so soon follow: students mentoring and comforting each other, keeping their rooms orderly and their possessions organized, and, most importantly, respecting each other's ideas and individual talents.

Creating a climate of personal respect and community extends to the parents at Gamble Montessori as well. Through personal dialogue and conferences, parents gradually realize that their children's teachers know their children intimately and care deeply about them, just as they as parents do. Teachers pattern their classrooms as inclusive environments for all learners, just as Montessori did, and look beyond misbehavior to see what the student might be trying to communicate through it, rather than immediately responding with punishments, even suspensions. As the authors write, you cannot help students if they are not even in the building. Parents respond to the caring and wisdom of their children's teachers and their ability to actually make a difference in their children's lives. It is with genuine gratitude that most parents develop a "sense of belonging" to their children's school community, too.

You may be thinking that all I have said sounds well and good, but what about academic standards? Actually, the authors make it very clear from their book's beginning that high standards are necessary in every aspect of human behavior and outcome—including academic knowledge. To not recognize this necessity would show a lack of respect for each individual child and his or her potential for development. Maintaining the highest standards for their students, however, does not mean minimizing the well-researched and documented difficulties encountered today in school systems throughout the country because of an overemphasis on constant standardized testing.

Teachers at Gamble Montessori must work within the test guidelines imposed upon them, but they are realistic about their usefulness to meaningful learning for their students. They find many ways to introduce choice and follow the students' interests in specific areas of learning, in addition to this enforced standardized curriculum. Much educational research supports this path to meaningful learning through choice and interest at every age, particularly in the formative years of childhood and adolescence.

One area that the Gamble Montessori teaching team has discovered is especially meaningful to high school students is the opportunity to leave the school walls behind and go out into the real world of adult life. These experiences are not the customary field trips organized in most schools. Rather, these are carefully structured meaningful experiences outside the classroom that are directly related to the students' studies and enhance them in deep and significant ways. For example, one structure for enhancing this goal of real-world learning is the establishment of Intersessions: expanded intense courses of study for credit in the fall and spring when students can choose from many topics presented. So successful are these courses that the authors state, "Real-world learning . . . must be at the heart of true educational reform."

It would be easy to read Jose's and Taylor's experiences as reported in *Angels and Superheroes* and think, "This cannot be real. Teenagers in such adverse circumstances cannot possibly be managing their lives this well." I certainly might have these thoughts myself if one bright fall day in October 2016, before this book was written, I and two of my Montessori teacher daughters had not happened to spend a morning at Gamble Montessori High School. We were shown around the school by three students who were proud, relaxed, talkative, and clearly in love with their school. We wandered into classrooms and through hallways. Some classrooms were empty, as a number of students were out of the building on those "real-world" experiences that day. Others were filled with students and teachers who were engaged and joyful. The culture of the school was clear. This was a place of love and of learning: an oasis of safety, peace, and trust.

We ended our visit with the principal in his inviting, relaxing, book-filled office. For almost an hour, Jose answered all our questions with warmth and enthusiasm. Yet I sensed that underneath his welcoming manner, he felt subdued. Eventually he explained that one of the Gamble students had committed suicide just two days before and grief was still raw, both for him personally and for the whole school community. When we parted outside the building on that fall day so gloriously filled with leaves of every color on ground and tree, Jose gave me a tender hug—my daughters told me later—with closed eyes and a gentle smile. I left, knowing that in one place on this earth, young teachers and their students are experiencing the triumph of the human spirit over tragedy and hardship in their everyday lives. It was a poignant day.

—Paula Polk Lillard, author of *Montesorri in the Classroom: A Teacher's Account of How Children Really Learn*

Acknowledgments

We originally thought of this book during a break at the very first conference presentation we ever gave together. It's quite possible that it started as a joke that sounded something like, "Hey, we should write a book about that!"

However, it was a joke rooted in a dream. A dream of sharing our stories with a wider audience and empowering teachers to trust in themselves and take risks to improve their practice.

That was in the fall of 2013. It took a lot of blood, sweat, and tears to bring this book to fruition, and we couldn't have done it without the support of many people.

To begin with, teaching isn't a profession that can be done in isolation. None of what we have shared in this text would have been possible without the incredible dedication of our colleagues at Gamble Montessori. The work they have done and the anecdotes they have shared show up throughout this book. They are the angels and superheroes of our story.

We also want to thank the many students who have passed through the classrooms and hallways of our schools. They have celebrated our successes and forgiven our failures as we have aspired to be the best educators we can be. It is they who have taught us everything we know about teaching.

Huge gratitude to Jonathan Reynolds, who spent many hours guiding us and answering our endless questions about the big, wide, scary world of publishing as we made our initial forays—and experienced our initial rejections—along the path of bringing this book to life.

Thanks, too, to Paul Wesselman (aka the Ripples Guy), who fortuitously found us on Facebook and decided to take us under his wing. His enthusiastic and unflappable cheerleading helped us to keep going when the going got tough, and his wise counsel helped us smooth our ruffled feathers when collaboration was hard.

And, of course, thanks to Sarah Jubar, our editor at Rowman & Littlefield, whose patience, hand-holding, and careful explanations of how things are done when one is writing a book were essential to making our dream a reality. Her concise edits and thoughtful feedback were the light that showed us the way.

JACK

Thanks to the countless mentors and coteachers who helped make me the educator I am today. I took a small part of each of you and nurtured it within me: Randy Boaz, you showed me that wonder is a transcendent human experience; Judy Mause, you showed me that seeing a child's full potential is the surest way to coax out his or her best effort; Bob Suess, you modeled hard work and showed me that compassion for others does not always mean hugging.

Thanks to the Westside Montessori staff who believed I could be principal and gave me the space to move from being their coworker to being their boss. In countless ways, you made a frightening change easier. And even now, as Gamble Montessori staff, I still strive daily to earn your trust and respect, and remember that I am a teacher first. Your stories fill these pages, often under pseudonyms.

Thanks, Mom. You always told me I could achieve my dream, whatever it was. Most importantly, you believed it. I am especially thankful for the night you told me, as our deadline approached, "I know writing a book is a long, tough slog. When you think you are done tonight, just do 10 more minutes. You can do it." If you are reading this, you were right, again.

Thank you, Krista. I swear this was all your idea and I was just going along with it. I am certain I *said* it was possible, but I didn't *believe* it the way you did. I just kept throwing my hat over the next wall and climbing over after it, and there you were beside me saying, "Isn't this great?" Yes, it is.

Thanks to Ben and Ellie, whose humor and patience with me are treasures I savor. I am afraid that I will always feel I never can spend enough time with you. Much of what I have done has been done to try and impress you, and prove that you can do all this and more. I believe in you.

Finally, thank you, Kathy. You are my rock. All of who I am and what I have done, I owe to you. Your steadfast dependability and selflessness are a clear reflection of your mother and grandmother, and I know they are proud. I strive every day to win your love and admiration. To quote the Indigo Girls, "One day I'm going to make it up to you . . . one day I'm coming home to stay, it's true."

KRISTA

Thanks to the teachers who taught me and the teachers who I have had the privilege of teaching alongside. When I think of the message of this book, you are the angels and superheroes I think of.

Particular thanks to my current teaching partners, Krista Mertens and Beau Wheatley. Throughout this process, you embraced my endless documentation of instructional best practices and obsessive pursuit of classroom anecdotes. The successes we have achieved with our students are in large part due to your dedication and commitment. I am so lucky to have each of you as coteachers.

Huge amounts of gratitude to my parents, Robert and Margaret Vitz. For decades, you have supported my work and dreams—no matter what form they have taken.

Big thanks to my children, Riley and Evan. You endured years of such responses as, "Not right now, I'm writing," or, "Don't talk, okay? I can't think when you talk." In some ways, this book was like a newborn that took all of your mother's attention. I am so grateful to you for your supportive comments, assuring me that the work I do matters and that my writing is important.

And I am hugely indebted to Blake. You read every word I wrote, often more than once, and provided stalwart personal support and the unfaltering conviction that the information in this book is valuable enough to share. In addition, and perhaps most importantly, throughout this process, you shouldered more than your share of the household and parenting responsibilities, and ensured that I was fed on a fairly regular basis. I am well aware that I could not do what I do without you standing beside me, believing in me, taking care of me, and listening to me talk about all of it for hours on end. Thank you for the gift of our life together.

Thanks as well to Jack, who walked through every part of this process with me, and without whom I would never have believed that any of this would have been possible.

Introduction

Dear teachers,

This book is for you. You are the unsung angels and capeless superheroes who walk among us. You are showing up in classrooms day after day, facing unprecedented challenges, one of which is an ever-expanding job description. This book is designed to support you in your efforts and help make your jobs more effective and fulfilling, and perhaps a little bit easier.

This book is for you because you have been under attack from the very people who should be your greatest supporters. The so-called school reform movement has targeted public schools, in general, and teachers, specifically, as "failing."

In October 2014, *TIME* magazine's cover story was about "Rotten Apples"—their metaphor for bad teachers. But you are not "rotten apples," and you are not failing. In fact, the data says something else entirely. It says that many teachers are up against the challenging foes of poverty and childhood trauma. The data also says that rather than failing, teachers are, overall, pretty successful.

Elected officials, who ought to be asking teachers what they want and need, and then seeking ways to provide it, are instead mandating accountability requirements that serve only to punish. Charter school lobbyists and other private interests have influenced the discussion at the highest levels, and the system has been turned upside-down from how it should be.

Few, if any, other countries' teachers do what American teachers do. American teachers educate every child for 13 years of public education in a society where economic disparity is profound, child poverty rates are high, and racial discrimination has a haunting and unresolved history. In this country, we educate every child regardless of ability, disability, economic status, or home environment.

American public education is perhaps the greatest contribution to democracy that exists. It is designed to be the great equalizer; however, school accountability efforts have moved education farther away from this goal rather than toward it. Despite the incredible pressures put on teachers by these evaluative laws, they continue to show up in their classrooms day after day, working as diligently as they can on behalf of their students.

Teaching is about so much more than what can be measured by any standardized test. While it is certainly about academic instruction, it is also about human growth and development, the cultivation of compassion and empathy, the establishment of trust and belonging, and the building of personal responsibility and societal advocacy. This is what is meant by educating the whole child. As teachers, we must meet students where they are and guide them toward becoming their best self, and we must be permitted and empowered to do so.

So, teachers, this book is for you.

We can't promise "Five Tips to Solve All Your Teaching Challenges," nor can we promise 10 tips, or even 25. Such a thing doesn't exist. Anyone who promises any variation of "Just Do These Things and Teaching Will Be Easy" is lying to you. Teaching is complex and complicated. Every class is unique. Every child is unique. There is never just one right way.

Instead, we have examined what has been most beneficial in our own practice and shared it here. The methodologies described are founded on research-based best practices supported by stories that exemplify the implementation of these strategies and the development of instruction that nurtures and respects the growth of the whole child. These are not fairy-tale stories of some perfect classroom where every day has a new happy ending. They are real stories about real teachers and real students figuring out how learning occurs in real classrooms. (Student and teacher identities are protected by the use of pseudonyms.)

These stories aren't our only stories. We have plenty of stories about when things didn't work out the way we had planned and success felt elusive. Those stories are the reality of the messy humanness of education. We all have those days that leave us wondering why we entered the field in the first place.

But those days are not what this book is about. This book is about the big-picture successes, each made up of an uncountable multitude of moments that remind us that teaching is the most noble profession in the world.

Some of the suggestions and ideas you read in this book will be right for you; some of them may not be. We suggest that rather than viewing this book as a tome to implement exactly as written, you read this book through the lens of your own experience. Consider which pieces are most applicable for your program, your classroom, and you. Don't try to tackle it all at once. Choose the area where you most want to focus and begin there.

Perhaps conversely, do not ignore those sections or chapters that make you feel uncomfortable. Consider that the feeling of discomfort may be an indicator of the places where you need to grow as an educator.

The most important thing is that you continue to examine your practice and make changes that lead you to more effective instruction. It's okay if this feels risky. Just like our students, if we're not making mistakes, we're not learning.

Once you have identified one or more of the concepts in this book that you want to implement, we recommend that you seek out others to join you in this work. When embarking on new journeys, it is helpful to identify people who will celebrate your successes with you and guide you through your failures. Both the successes and failures are an important part of developing new techniques and strategies. Both are crucial parts of the process.

Consider forming a support group of sorts. Find a group of teachers who have self-selected to work on implementing similar changes. Designate a consistent meeting time where you can share successes and challenges with one another and work collaboratively to research best practices to deepen and enrich your instruction.

This can be a very powerful forum for inspiration, sustenance, and support, especially if it is conducted on an "opt-in" basis. As such, everyone present wants to be there and has chosen to engage in the work in this way. Approach your administrator about awarding professional development hours for your time together. After all, there is no more powerful professional development than that which has been identified as valuable by the participants involved and self-designed to meet those needs.

During a time in education where it can feel like so much is outside our control and so many requirements are not aligned with the passion that drove us to the field in the first place, it is imperatuve that teachers reclaim the type of work that nurtures students and reinvigorates learning. That is the focus of our book.

Collectively, Jack and I have taught gifted students, English-language learners, and students with severe behavioral disorders and other learning challenges. We have taught in wealthy suburbs and impoverished cities in Ohio for more than 30 years combined.

At Gamble Montessori, in Cincinnati Public Schools, where we have worked together for eight years, we have experienced the roller-coaster ride of both crushing budget cuts and large federal grants. On the Ohio State Report Card, Gamble Montessori has been rated as "effective" and "excellent" and has earned three consecutive "A" grades in "value added." It has also been rated as having made "continuous improvement" and "earned" multiple "F" scores in performance and achievement, including "value added."

We have felt the sting of how political decisions can make a successful school—one where students enjoy coming to school, love learning, and take on the challenges of both schoolwork and social justice issues—look like a failing school. And we have fought the embarrassment of making this "grade card" the most public description of our school.

We know that the primary change that occurred during this apparent decline was in educational law, not in the practices and performance of the students and staff. We know that every class brings its own set of challenges to school and that every group of teachers brings time, passion, and hundreds of their own dollars into their classrooms to create the best learning opportunities for students. And we know that we are not alone in this experience.

We write to say this: Take heart. Your work matters. Every child who walks into your classroom is important and will benefit from your love and preparation. The reason you became a teacher has not changed. Your value is enhanced, not diminished, in these times.

The children in our classrooms can't be bid out to the cheapest substitute. They deserve better than that. We have outlived and outwitted even tougher opponents than legislators, and we are currently in the process of educating the next group of politicians. These children will be seated in front of you, maybe even today or tomorrow. Teach them well.

Take heart. You are brave. You are up to the challenge. To us, and to your students, you are an angel; you are a superhero.

Read on to discover how to shine your halo and strengthen your superpowers. It's time to save the soul of education. Your students are counting on you.

Sincerely,
Krista and Jack

1

The Problem, the Solution, and Our Goal

Imagine a standardized test being used to measure the healing of a patient and the effectiveness of the doctor. It would look something like this: A doctor sees a patient through treatment of a condition, and at the end of a prescribed length of time, the patient completes a multiple-choice, fill-in-the-bubble test to determine progress. It is irrelevant what the patient's condition was at the start of treatment, what other issues the patient is experiencing, how long the patient received treatment, or how well the patient followed medical advice.

The physician's perception of the patient's progress, or any additional insights he or she might have, is also irrelevant. It is the test result that will determine whether the physician is an effective practitioner and the patient has made sufficient progress.

The scenario above is readily recognized as absurd, and even potentially dangerous, when applied to medicine. So why is it so widely accepted as appropriate for education? In the given scenario, substitute "student" for "patient" and "teacher" for "doctor," and this is exactly how teaching and learning are being measured. Yet, education is nearly as complex and individualized a process as medicine.

However, in the United States, high-stakes standardized testing is commonly viewed as not only appropriate for education, but also essential. It is deemed so essential that, even in the face of dissent from the majority of parents and educators, politicians continue to reinforce the myth that standardized tests are a fundamental method for assessing student learning and, therefore, by extrapolation, a credible way to determine the effectiveness of teachers and schools.

This false narrative was initiated with the publication of *A Nation at Risk* in 1983, and reinforced and perpetuated through such legislation as Goals 2000, No Child Left Behind (NCLB), Race to the Top, and, most recently, the Every Student Succeeds Act.

THE PROBLEM

Politicians and the media have had a field day "exposing" and attempting to address what has been described as an "educational crisis" in the United States. In the rush to quantify, evaluate, and ostensibly improve our educational system, the United States has forgotten that education is complicated and that any attempt to distill it into a simplistic measure will fall short—and compromise the nobility of the work.

There is a growing body of evidence indicating that this supposed "crisis" in American education has been misreported and that this myth of decline has been supported and sustained by a repeated skewing of the data. Layers of punitive accountability measures have been added to teachers' already overflowing plates. This has come primarily in the form of standardized testing of students, with the results used to evaluate public schools, their teachers, and entire districts.

As a result of this, educators throughout the country are desperately trying to protect the soul of education—the nurturance and development of the whole child. It is teachers who are on the front lines of this battle, and they are engaged in a fight that must be waged both offensively and defensively.

As an offensive approach, teachers must understand what exactly it is they are up against, and they must collectively speak out against this. Simultaneously, they must defensively seek to create classrooms that push against the focus on testing outcomes and instead support the needs of the children within them. This is not an easy mission, but it is one that educators throughout the country are desperate to engage in as a means of reclaiming the heart of the honorable profession they have chosen.

THE RESEARCH

Although it has been widely publicized that the American public school system is experiencing a decline, there is long-term evidence that refutes this claim. The National Assessment of Educational Progress (NAEP) is a nationwide database that has tracked student progress in reading and math since the early 1970s. The assessments used to collect this information have been carefully monitored for consistency for almost 40 years. These tests are given to students throughout the country at ages 9, 13, and 17. The results of this data indicate that reading and math scores have remained fairly static from year to year, with both increasing somewhat over time. For example, the 2012 data indicated that for 13-year-olds, the average reading scores increased by eight raw points and average math scores increased by 21 raw points since the first data was reported in 1978.[1]

This does not look like a crisis at all. The "educational crisis" hysteria has seemed to predominantly come from information comparing U.S. educational data with that from other countries.

When we compare educational outcomes, we must be careful to monitor for external factors—for example, when comparing data internationally, we must take into account that the United States educates and assesses students until the age of 18, whereas some other countries place students in various forms of tracked models and do not include all of these groups in their testing.

Additionally, the United States has a high child poverty rate. The 2012 United Nations Children's Fund (UNICEF) report listed the U.S. child poverty rate as 34th out of 35 "economically advanced" countries, with only Romania scoring lower (see Table 1.1).[2]

We know that poverty impacts academic achievement, and this must be taken into account when comparing U.S. scores internationally. For example, when the oft-cited data from the Program for International Assessment

Table 1.1. UNICEF Relative Child Poverty* in 35 Economically Advanced Countries

Iceland	4.7
Finland	5.3
Cyprus	6.1
Netherlands	6.1
Norway	6.1
Slovenia	6.3
Denmark	6.5
Sweden	7.3
Austria	7.3
Czech Republic	7.4
Switzerland	8.1
Ireland	8.4
Germany	8.5
France	8.8
Malta	8.9
Belgium	10.2
Hungary	10.3
Australia	10.9
Slovakia	11.2
New Zealand	11.7
Estonia	11.9
United Kingdom	12.1
Luxembourg	12.3
Canada	13.3
Poland	14.5
Portugal	14.7
Japan	14.9
Lithuania	15.4
Italy	15.9
Greece	16.0
Spain	17.1
Bulgaria	17.8
Latvia	18.8
United States	**23.1**
Romania	25.5

*Relative child poverty defined as percent of children, ages 0 to 17, living in households with equivalent income lower than 50% of the national median when adjusted for family size and composition.

Source: Peter Adamson, *Measuring Child Poverty: New League Tables of Child Poverty in the World's Rich Countries, UNICEF Office of Research,* May 2012. Retrieved June 3, 2017, from www.unicef-irc.org/publications/pdf/rc10_eng.pdf.

(PISA) is disaggregated based on economic status, we can see a trend that clearly indicates that the problem is poverty, rather than quality of instruction.

Based on the 2009 PISA data, U.S. schools with less than 10% of students living in poverty score higher on these tests than any other country in the world. Schools with student poverty rates that are less than 24.9% rank third in the world, and schools with poverty rates ranging from 25% to 49.9% rank 10th in the world; however, schools with 50% to 74.9% poverty rates rank much lower—fifth from the bottom. Tragically, schools with 75% or higher poverty rates rank lower in reading scores than any country except Mexico (see Table 1.2).[3]

Couple this with 2013 data that indicates that a majority (51%) of public school students live in poverty in this country, and we see the true depth of the actual problem of poverty and its impact on education.[4] The United States has an excellent comprehensive public educational system that struggles with a poverty problem that originates far beyond the walls of the classroom. The problem isn't schools, or teachers, or students. The problem is poverty.

The Problem of Poverty

The disaggregated PISA results demonstrate what has been shown time and time again: Schools with the lowest rates of student achievement are typically those with the highest number of disadvantaged students and the fewest available resources. The problem runs deeper than just funding, however. Children living in poverty often have a specialized set of social–emotional and academic needs. Schools with high percentages of economically disadvantaged students cannot be treated in the same manner as more affluent schools.

Children living in poverty are more likely to be coping with what has been labeled "toxic stress"—caused by a high number of identified adverse childhood events. Such factors as death or incarceration of a parent, addiction, mental illness, and abuse, among other things, have been labeled as adverse childhood events. Poverty, itself, is considered to be a type of sustained adverse childhood experience, and it also is a correlate factor, since living in poverty increases the likelihood of experiencing other adverse childhood events.[5]

These types of severe and chronic stress lead to long-term changes in children's mental and physical development, and this directly impacts their performance in school.

> On an emotional level, toxic stress can make it difficult for children to moderate their responses to disappointments and provocations. A highly sensitive stress-response system constantly on the lookout for threats can produce patterns of behavior that are self-defeating in school: fighting, talking back, acting

Table 1.2. Average 2009 PISA Scores on Combined Literacy Scale by Country*

Country	*Score*
U.S. schools with less than 10% of students eligible for the federal lunch program	**551**
Republic of Korea	539
Finland	536
Hong Kong, China	533
U.S. schools with 10% to 24.9% of students eligible for the federal lunch program	**527**
Singapore**	526
Canada	524
New Zealand	521
Japan	520
Australia	515
Netherlands	508
Belgium	506
Norway	503
U.S. schools with 25% to 49.9% of students eligible for the federal lunch program	**502**
Estonia	501
Switzerland	501
Poland	500
Iceland	500
U.S. average	**500**
Lichtenstein**	499
Sweden	497
Germany	497
Ireland	496
Chinese Taipei**	495
France	496
Denmark	495
United Kingdom	494
Hungary	494
Portugal	489
Macao, China**	487
Italy	486
Latvia	484
Slovenia	483
Greece	483
Spain	481
Czech Republic	478
Slovak Republic	477
Croatia**	472
Israel	474
Luxembourg	472
U.S. schools with 50% to 74.9% of students eligible for the federal lunch program	**471**
Austria	470
Lithuania**	468
Turkey	464

Country	*Score*
Dubai, United Arab Emirates**	459
Russian Federation	459
Chile	449
U.S. schools with 75% to 100% of students eligible for the federal lunch program	**446**
Republic of Serbia**	442
Bulgaria**	429
Uruguay**	426
Mexico	425
There are 17 non-OECD countries that fall below Mexico's rating	424–314

*Combined results for Organization for Economic Cooperation and Development (OECD) and non-OECD countries. U.S. data disaggregated by school socioeconomic averages. Shanghai's results have been removed from this table due to concerns about accurate population sampling.
**Indicates a non-OECD country.
Source: U.S. Department of Education, *Highlights from PISA 2009: Performance of U.S. 15-Year-Old Students in Reading, Mathematics, and Science Literacy in an International Context, National Center for Education Statistics*, 2010. Retrieved December 20, 2016, from https://nces.ed.gov/pubs2011/2011004.pdf.

> up, and, more subtly, going through each day perpetually wary of connection with peers or teachers. On a cognitive level, chronically elevated stress can disrupt the development of what are known as executive functions, . . . which include working memory, attentional control, and cognitive flexibility.[6]

Children living in poverty face greater academic challenges than their middle- and upper-class counterparts. Yet, instead of helping this situation, the school accountability movement has chosen to vilify the wrong thing (teachers and schools) and use standardized test scores as the weapon of choice to add insult to injury.

The crisis the U.S. education system is facing is not the failure of teachers and schools to educate children. The myth of a failing public school system has led to the creation of a "school reform" movement, and, in turn, this "reform" effort has deeply woven the testing industry into the fabric of American education. The actual crisis lies with these "reform" efforts themselves.

Hidden Costs

The school accountability—or school "reform"—movement has mandated standardized testing and directly ties the results of these tests to the evaluation of schools, teachers, and students. Prior to the implementation of NCLB, the U.S. Department of Education mandated six standardized tests. This number increased to 14 after NCLB was enacted. And in the rush to quantify and measure, states and districts have added additional testing requirements, such that between kindergarten and 12th grade, the average student will take 113 standardized tests.[7]

For schools, test scores are reflected in published ratings, and these results have negatively impacted funding for schools that did not meet the goals set for them. For teachers, test data often comprises part of performance reviews. This can lead to job insecurity and, in some schools, can influence salaries. For students, test results can determine promotion and graduation. The potential consequences of testing outcomes are important for all parties involved.

The U.S. public school system has become overly focused on this single measurement of success, and that measure is most punitive to populations that are already struggling. In 2013, the American Federation of Teachers (AFT) reported that in heavily tested grades, as many as 50 hours a year were spent on testing and as many as 110 hours a year were devoted to test preparation.[8] Schools with high percentages of disadvantaged students bear the greatest weight for this, as they tend to have the greatest required gains in testing outcomes—and the stakes are high. The Center for American Progress notes that students in urban high schools spend as much as 266% more time taking standardized tests than students in suburban schools.[9]

Student Costs

This increased focus on measurable cognitive outcomes has hidden costs for all students. By definition, all norm-referenced assessments are designed to fail—or deem as "not proficient"—a predetermined portion of test takers. This means that these tests are intentionally crafted to ensure that some students are unsuccessful. These are often the same students, year after year. This creates a sense of futility in students as they develop negative perceptions about themselves and their ability to learn and fosters suspicion of the system in which they continue to "fail."

In addition, the testing frenzy and the many hours it requires leaves little time for the development of such so-called soft skills as curiosity, perseverance, conscientiousness, and sociability. Yet, it is these skills that may have the greatest positive long-term outcomes. Seventy-seven percent of employers say that soft skills, such as integrity, communication, responsibility, flexibility, and teamwork, are equally important to content-related skills.[10]

School accountability measures, with their fundamental focus on testing, reduce teachers' ability to focus on nurturing students' noncognitive abilities, and this is perhaps irrevocably damaging. Education has become obsessed with a culture of data. We have data talks, data folders, data meetings, and even data rooms. We classify students by test scores and colors. Many teachers have heard the advice to focus on "yellow" students—those students whose data points indicate that they are near the cusp of "proficiency." No need to worry about the green students, as they are likely to pass the test regardless of further instruction. And the red students? Well, they're a bit of a lost cause, so no need to worry about them either. This shift away from a learner-centered focus and toward an outcome-centered focus is changing society's understanding of the fundamental purpose of education and the value of the individual child. This system has negative ramifications, not only for the "red" students, but also for the "green" ones.

Teacher Costs

There is a second set of hidden costs to the school reform movement's focus on testing and accountability. The United States is rapidly moving toward a teacher shortage. As the reach and influence of testing and testing preparation have expanded, students are being dehumanized and teachers are being deprofessionalized. The role and function of teachers are changing as educators lose authority and autonomy over instruction due to mandated curricula, pacing, and guidelines designed to prepare students for testing.

The stress and exhaustion of teaching are well documented. A recent Gallup poll indicates that 46% of teachers experience high levels of daily stress. This is on par with nurses and tops the list of surveyed occupations.[11] Continual stress and exhaustion lead to burnout, but teacher burnout is more than just a problem for individual teachers and schools. It is so pervasive that it has profound impacts on the profession as a whole.

NPR cites the following concerning statistics:

A total of 8% of teachers leave the field each year; only one-third of this attrition is due to retirement.

Some 50% of the teaching profession turns over every seven years

Approximately 40% to 50% of teachers leave the profession within the first five years.

> Enrollment in teacher-training programs has fallen 35% in the past five years, a loss of 240,000 teachers.[12]

Teaching has never been an easy job, but the greatest challenge of teaching should be educating the students in the classroom. That is a tremendously difficult job all by itself for a wide variety of reasons. When this work is made harder by policies, inefficiencies, and bureaucracy, all parties involved—teachers, students, parents—have been done a grave disservice.

And, yet, the increased pressures and requirements brought about by high-stakes standardized testing, accountability measures, and school reform have done just that. The 2012 MetLife Survey of the American Teacher noted that only 39% of teachers feel satisfied with their jobs. The same question asked in 2008 indicated that 62% of teachers felt satisfied with their jobs. This indicates a decline of 23% in just four years, four years in which accountability requirements increased.

Students and teachers are being negatively impacted by testing and accountability measures; it seems that perhaps the only group for which these so-called reform efforts are beneficial is made up of the testing companies themselves, and they are profiting wildly.

Hidden Profits

According to the National Board of Educational Testing and Public Policy, in 1955 standardized test sales totaled about $7 million annually. By 1997, that number had increased to $263 million—an increase of more than 3,000%.[13]

In 2012, the Brookings Institution determined that approximately $669 million was directly spent on the purchase of assessments in 45 states. In 2014–2015, the state of Ohio spent approximately $142 million on the purchase and administration of the standard battery of required tests alone.[14] This figure doesn't include the cost of testing retake sessions, costs to districts for administrative coordination of testing, or expenses incurred through the purchase and use of test prep materials.

The market for these tests is huge. According to the National Center for Education Statistics, there are 98,454 public schools in the United States, serving approximately 50.4 million students. Requiring testing in every public school in the country creates a gigantic captive market.

Three companies, CTB McGraw-Hill, Houghton Mifflin, Harcourt, and Pearson, essentially control this market. Pearson is the largest of these corporations, bringing in more than $9 billion annually.[15]

There is indeed big money to be made, but high-stakes standardized testing is not just an innocuous moneymaking endeavor. It is damaging to schools, teachers, and students alike. Here is one example of how out of control testing has become.

At Gamble Montessori, Bryce is a student with an identified learning disability. He struggles academically but performs especially poorly in a testing situation.

Bryce is now a junior in high school, and he has not yet passed any of the tests required for high school graduation in the state of Ohio. There are seven of these—ELA I, ELA II, algebra I, geometry (or integrated math I), biology, American history, and American government. Each test has two sections. Extended testing time is written into Bryce's IEP, so he must be provided with the option of using the entire day to complete each section of each test. He is a student who needs this extra time.

When all of this is taken into consideration—seven tests of two sections each and one day designated to take each test—it amounts to 14 school days (or almost three weeks) of testing. Consider also that Bryce was expected to take six of these state tests during the first round of retakes in December (two sections for each test, so 12 days), as well as taking the ACT in April.

In sum, had his school complied with state and district requirements for testing, he would have spent almost 30 days—or the equivalent of six weeks of the school year—taking tests. This is not just some crazy nightmare; this is Bryce's current reality.

Huge Costs, Little Gain

This is madness. Ultimately, this testing epidemic is not even about student learning. Rather, it is about assessment of public teachers and public schools. The test results that we put so much stake in and spend so much time thinking about and preparing for are of little use for instructing students.

The preliminary test results are generally released throughout the summer, and final data is usually provided at some point in the fall. At this point, the students who took these tests have moved on—to a new grade, a new teacher, and a new curriculum. The tests they will take next will be focused on the expectations of the new curriculum, not the old one, so knowing a student's scores from the prior year is only marginally beneficial for a teacher.

In addition, what does this data show? It may seem as if this question should have an obvious answer. They show what a student knows; therefore, by extrapolation, they show how well a student has been taught. But this assumption implies that teachers are unable to appropriately assess student learning without these assessments and that the data these tests generate is valid.

Most teachers' test scores vary from year to year—sometimes wildly. If test scores demonstrate effective teaching, annual score variance would subsequently indicate that any given teacher's instruction is markedly better or worse depending on the year. It is unlikely that a teacher's skills would fluctuate that dramatically from year to year, especially given that, ostensibly, instructional skills increase with additional experience and practice.

Education is neither a business nor a factory. Unlike in a factory, teachers and schools do not start with identical raw materials and act upon them in a systematic way to produce an identical product. In the same vein, unlike in a factory, instructional efficacy cannot be judged in a single manner, with a single measure, and be expected to have a consistent result. Teaching is a service industry, and teachers work with humans.

Moreover, there has been a lot of discussion about the merits of evaluating proficiency versus, or in tandem with, growth. Proficiency measures student learning relative to an anticipated outcome, whereas growth measures student learning relative to a baseline, or the point from which the student started. Most educators find growth to be a better descriptor of student learning than proficiency; however, attempting to quantify this growth through tests is problematic.

These growth measures (often called value-added scores) can indicate huge gains—more than two years of academic growth in a year's time. That sounds great, but is this plausible? Does it make sense that, in the course of a year, a student could more than double the amount of learning expected to occur?

In the same vein, value-added measures can indicate huge losses—more than two years of academic decline in a year's time. How is this even remotely possible? How is it possible for a teacher to be so bad that she or he causes a student to lose two years of academic instruction, while simultaneously providing instruction for an entire year? This simply isn't reasonable. These commonsense arguments aren't the only rationale against value-added data; statisticians are unconvinced as well.

There is a tremendous lack of transparency concerning how these measures are calculated and whether they are even valid.[16] This has been repeatedly called into question. Yet this data continues to be used to measure the effectiveness of public education. It is also intriguing that these school accountability measures have not expanded beyond the public school sector.

If standardized test data truly does tell us such important information, why aren't private and parochial schools demanding the use of these assessment tools? Why aren't politicians and other private school parents requesting that the schools many of their children attend use these tests to measure student learning and teacher effectiveness? Don't they want the best for their children? Don't they want to be reassured that their child is learning? Don't they want to know the quality of their children's teachers? Don't they want this same data?

No, they don't. They don't insist on equal testing because standardized tests are not an effective tool for assessing these important things. Students in public schools are put through this wringer of testing for what? If it provides little information about kids, little information about instruction, and little information about teachers, what is its purpose?

Parents and educators are up against a mighty foe—the testing industry—and a social construct that school accountability measures are effective, necessary, and appropriate.

Today's teachers are desperately searching for a way to do everything that is being asked of them, while still hanging on to the heart of education that drew them to the field in the first place: the nurturing of children, the development of wonder, the thrill of the aha moment, the creation of a curious and informed populace. How can teachers continue to do this incredibly challenging and important work in an environment that can be so difficult, stultifying, and, at times, downright damaging?

Saving the soul of education will require that teaching and learning be examined through a different lens. As a society, we must stop punishing teachers through these "reform" efforts and instead trust teachers, as highly trained professionals, to work in the best interest of each child.

THE SOLUTION

There are no simple quick-fix solutions. The antieducation "school reform" movement is powerful. It will take time to weaken its death grip on the throat of public schools. Saving education by fighting the dehumanization occurring through the school accountability movement is an act of resistance. This resistance must take place both outside and inside the classroom.

External Focus

Outside the classroom, teachers must begin making their voices heard. The field of education has been systematically undermined by a repeated and unsupported message that public education is failing and that teachers are lazy and ineffective. This leads to a disempowerment of teachers, such that their input and perspective are discounted.

Educators must reclaim their power, their voice, and their expertise. They must insist on being heard—not just as a voice in the conversation, but also as the most influential voice in the conversation. There is no one more aware of the needs and challenges in the classroom than teachers. Teachers remain the preeminent experts on teaching.

Teachers are highly educated professionals and should be treated as such. A single test measure can never tell teachers more about students than what they already know from their day-to-day instruction. Teachers are highly practiced in assessment, observation, and interpretation of results, which, when conducted over the course of a year, are far better reflections of student learning than any standardized test result.

Teachers must also reach out to parents. There are few parents who are in favor of the current focus on testing in schools. Research indicates that the majority of parents are happy with their child's teacher and school. Parents want to support education, but they often don't know how. What is it that teachers need? What is in the best interest of the children in the classroom?

Teachers are often expected to be politically neutral, and there is generally an unspoken expectation that teachers and school administrators should not rock the district, state, or federal boat regarding educational policies, and certainly should not incite parents to do the same. There can be repercussions for teachers who do so.

The acceptance of this type of suffocating bullying has led education down the dead-end road where it is now stuck, trapped in place by legislation and the profiteering of the testing industry. Educators must be the voice of resistance. Like physicians, if the pledge is to, "First do no harm," teachers can no longer be passive. Our students are suffering.

Education is complicated. Student growth is broad and deep, and sometimes happens in fits and starts, while at other times it develops slowly and consistently. This complex process could never be adequately measured by a series of tests.

To assume that a testing company could determine student learning and make judgments on the effectiveness of a teacher's instruction based solely on a single measure is folly—especially when students in poverty, the teachers who educate them, and the schools that serve them will be judged most harshly by these measures. In fact, standardized test scores may tell us little about a teacher's impact or a student's future success.

Internal Focus

As Paul Tough, author of *How Children Succeed*, writes,

> A few years ago, a young economist at Northwestern University named C. Kirabo Jackson began investigating how to measure educators' effectiveness. In many school systems these days, teachers are assessed based primarily on one data point: the standardized test scores of their students. Jackson suspected that the true impact teachers had on their students was more complicated than a single test score could reveal. . . . He created a proxy measure for students' noncognitive ability. Jackson's new index measured how engaged students were in school—whether they showed up, whether they misbehaved, and how hard they worked in their classes. Jackson found that this was, remarkably, a better predictor than student's test scores of whether the students would go on to attend college, a better predictor of adult wages, and a better predictor of future arrests."[17]

This should not come as a surprise. It seems as if nearly everyone can readily name one or more teachers who had a profound influence on their growth and development. When asked to identify this teacher's strengths, invariably it is a focus on the noncognitive skills that emerges—teachers who pushed students to never give up, helped students believe in themselves, taught acceptance and inclusivity, or helped students find self-respect and dignity. Teachers who taught students to believe in themselves and their own potential.

Now consider the impossibility of designing a standardized test–based teacher- or school-evaluation system centered on fostering *those* qualities. Teachers in the United States are desperately seeking ways to build educational institutions around the growth and development of children, instead of test scores. There is no quick fix that creates this nurturing relationship, just as there is no single data point that can measure it. Rather, this is built through an investment in, and commitment to, being present, paying attention, maintaining consistency, engaging in hard work, practicing humility, and working together.

The current accountability culture has discounted the importance of growth and learning beyond the construct of the mythic test, and this devaluing of the student–teacher relationship into nothing more than a numbers game is a sickness. Teachers must be allowed to reclaim the nobility of the profession, and this must begin at the classroom level with a return to a focus on the unique and individual needs of each child. Educators are working hard to try to maintain and rekindle joy in learning in the face of testing pressures.

CONCLUSION

Teachers, administrators, parents, and students are experiencing concern and anxiety regarding how to implement the current accountability requirements, while still holding on to the soul of education—nurturing the growth of the child and adolescent.

The educational philosophers, politicians, and statisticians of the reform movement have forgotten about the real people involved: the children who come to school every day carrying an untold number of stressors and the adults who arrive each morning with big dreams and bigger hearts, desperately wishing to be the angels and superheroes these children need.

Contrary to popular opinion about the role of teachers in the story of education today, we are not currently experiencing an epidemic of angels with tarnished halos and superheroes with torn capes. Rather, these angels and superheroes are desperately trying to find a way to do it all.

They are trying to protect their jobs and schools by jumping through the hoops (and sometimes, seemingly, over tall buildings in a single bound), while still managing to serve the fallible humans, the students, whose needs are so tangible and real. Without effort to address the hoops, standards, and goals, it is unlikely that these teachers will have a job; without effort to address the needs of the individual students they serve, it is unlikely that they will have any incentive to go to work each day.

This dichotomy has led to a sometimes seemingly insurmountable challenge. How do teachers continue to do the incredibly demanding work of education in an environment that can be so difficult, stultifying, and, at times, downright damaging? How can educators find a way to effectively meet all the expectations placed on them and simultaneously nurture the children in their care? This is the crisis contemporary educators are facing, but there are implementable solutions.

The remaining chapters in this book explore extensions and shifts in practice and classroom climate that can connect the dots and serve as an antidote to the demoralizing impact of the era of accountability that is stifling the heart and soul of education. Each chapter provides a different lens through which to examine how to resist the lure—or, in many cases, the mandate—of teaching to the test and explores how to make classrooms places of vibrant instruction and learning.

TIPS OF THE TRADE

- Be a voice in the conversation. Have confidence in your expertise and discuss the issues in education with everyone and anyone who will listen.
- Support your colleagues. Encourage one another in making classrooms places of joy and learning where test preparation and test results matter less than student needs.
- Insist on instruction that meets students where they are and moves them forward in a manner that is student-friendly and engaging. Resist inappropriate standards, curriculum, and pacing.
- Advocate for wraparound services in schools. The neediest students require more support than can be provided simply through classroom instruction.
- Refuse to be silenced.
- Read the rest of this book.

OVERVIEW

Chapter 2: Creating a Culture for Academic Respect and High Standards

Creating clear definitions of what a student should be able to do in a given academic class is the foundation for building accountability to high standards. One strategy to avoid a seemingly random smattering of unrelated concepts is to develop thematic units, using key standards from the curriculum. Understanding the relationship between standards and the overarching ideas that tie together different disciplines and classes helps create a rationale for learning that paves the way to greater student involvement and improved learning through greater retention of information.

Standards are not always measurable objectives with numbers and letters. In fact, the highest standards we set for one another include integrity, honesty, and setting challenging expectations for ourselves. Benjamin Zander said, "Never doubt the capacity of the people you lead to accomplish whatever you dream for them." The highest standard is achieving our dreams.

Chapter 3: Building a Caring and Supportive Community in the Classroom and Beyond

Community is at the core of a successful academic environment. Oftentimes, however, creating community is viewed as a by-product of teaching and learning—something that happens as a natural outcome of instruction, rather than something that is carefully crafted through intentional community building, and that, in turn, actually creates the environment in which effective teaching and learning can occur.

Such practices as the establishment of cohesive groupings, student looping, and intentional community development with staff, parents, and the community as a whole help develop and strengthen learning communities in all their variations to promote a stable and healthy institution, develop resilience in students, and enhance student academic and behavioral outcomes.

Chapter 4: Creating a Climate of Interpersonal Respect

Many schools struggle to meet the needs of their minority students both academically and culturally. Tenets of "sameness" and "color blindness" do not serve the child who feels left out during ceremonies and classroom discussions about something the teacher assumes everyone understands.

Learning occurs best in an environment where each student and staff member feels accepted for who they are and then is willing to make mistakes. Children are eager to learn about themselves, and this exploration is well started by building on their desire to learn about others.

Building racially and culturally welcoming language into policies and procedures, and overtly teaching not only tolerance, but also an appreciation for what is different, is not just a nice idea, but also a strategy for improved creativity and success in problem-solving.

Chapter 5: Discovering How Misbehavior Reveals Unmet Needs

Behavior management is often cited by teachers as the most challenging component of teaching; student misbehavior can result in the loss of significant instructional time. Common school-based responses to misbehavior involve consequences and punishment. While these may provide short-term solutions, they do little to impart long-term behavioral change.

The development of proactive classroom management strategies supports teachers and students in examining and addressing students' underlying needs and thus eliciting real behavioral change. By maintaining an objective viewpoint, resisting the natural reaction of personalizing student misbehavior, and intentionally addressing unmet needs, teachers can create a positive classroom environment that is conducive to learning.

Chapter 6: Designing Instruction to Create an Inclusive Environment for All Learners

Today's classrooms reflect the diversity found in American society better than ever before. Learning alongside what may have once been considered "typical students" are English-language learners, gifted students, students with disabilities, and students from a wide range of home situations and cultural backgrounds. This comes with many inherent challenges, but it also comes with an equal number of tremendous blessings.

With classes that are invariably comprised of students with a wide range of needs and abilities, many schools use tracking of students as a strategy for addressing these differences; however, this methodology is being challenged as being shortsighted in addressing the needs of the whole child.

A diverse classroom can provide the richest learning environment for all learners, and teachers need strategies for how to effectively instruct learners at all levels. Additionally, students are most powerfully engaged when they are able to make choices about how to demonstrate their learning.

Chapter 7: Using Real-World Experiences to Enhance Learning

One important purpose of a school is to prepare students for the "real world" of work. The traditional school and classroom model prepares students to do what they are told and move on cue—perfect skills for the kinds of jobs that are disappearing. School and teacher evaluation have made high-stakes testing a cornerstone of national education conversation, and most districts and schools have responded in a predictable fashion—by shortening recess at elementary schools, reducing the number of fine arts electives available to students, and eliminating field trips and guest speakers.

However, the best learning—the learning that transforms the child—often occurs outside the classroom. Real-world learning not only prepares students for the "real world," but also enhances their memory and creates greater engagement, and must be at the heart of true educational reform.

Chapter 8: Practicing What You Preach: Using Modeling to Effect Real Change

Empty platitudes from leadership are the source of much humor because it is so common in workplaces for managers to violate the very principles they are supposed to uphold. In every aspect of the job, how a principal interacts with staff at times when things don't go according to plan—sick days, missed deadlines, teaching mistakes, miscommunication with parents—determines how the staff will respond to similar errors by students. A 2012 Gates Foundation survey of more than 10,000 teachers found that 68% stated supportive leadership as "absolutely essential" in their decision to remain at a school or in the profession at all.

Through a mix of intentional participation in specially designed professional development and well-intentioned efforts at self-improvement, administrators can model and mentor the personal and professional growth they seek from their teachers.

2

Creating a Culture for Academic Respect and High Standards

A child yearns to use the precise tools and language associated with each new skill he or she encounters. As evidence, one adolescent reported on his recent babysitting episode. The six-year-old he was watching insisted that they play Pokémon for much of their time together. Pokémon is a card game where players accrue cards featuring pictures and a range of statistics for various characters, collectively called Pokémon.

Players draw the cards from their decks, and the Pokémon engage in a battle far more complex than the classic playing card game War, involving details from the statistics on the card interacting in different ways depending on the characteristics of each Pokémon. It is very intricate, as this adolescent found out.

"He knew every card," said the adolescent. "He knew their names, which attacks they could perform." He shrugged his shoulders and laughed about his misfortune in game after game, adding, "I won a game at the end, but I am pretty sure it is because he let me." The six-year-old had studied his cards and independently mastered a new set of technical terms and complex rules for a card game many adults find mystifying.

He exhibited a stunning level of not only comprehension of the game and the names of the characters, but also detailed memories of the characteristics, including sets of numbers in various categories. Often, he would accurately predict the result of a series of actions that, to his babysitter, seemed a complete mystery.

This is not the experience of a genius child prodigy. Rather, it is the fairly common experience of almost all parents of children at that age. They love to learn. They love precise language. They yearn to experiment.

And then something happens to them that makes them stop loving to learn.

THE PROBLEM

Set within the confines of a "factory model" school are system after system designed with the same idea in mind: Make it as easy as possible for the teachers and administrators to process children in through the front door of kindergarten and out the other side, whether holding a diploma, a GED, or a grudge against a system that failed them. This factory model has been tweaked, of course, since its implementation and prodigious growth in the late 1800s, with each structure of refinement put in place throughout the years offering an opportunity to respect, or disrespect, students and the learning process.

The physical structure of the classroom, systems of grouping students, grading systems, and even the curriculum itself have been changed multiple times by individuals at the federal, state, and local levels. Each change, at any of these levels, can serve to either empower or enfeeble the student. Ultimately, the final decision sits in the hands of the teacher in the classroom, to shield the student from the negative changes and prepare him or her for the positive ones.

The academic system was designed to provide specific sets of information to students in the most direct and efficient way possible. Large, theater-style classrooms, with seats bolted to the floor and facing the front of the classroom, supported this "sit and get" approach. A teacher would stand at the front of the room and pour out knowledge for the students to take in. Her role was clear: Dispense information and pass judgment on student progress. These rows of bolted-down chairs were later replaced with individual desks, which could, in appropriate but still rare circumstances, be rotated into group conversations.

Because the industrialized model was meant to efficiently identify and sort out the college-bound from the factory-bound, grading served not so much to measure growth as to differentiate the "best" students from the "worst," with a general expectation that the final grades were distributed evenly along a bell curve. Most students were average, the reasoning went. Teachers with "too many" As or Fs were questioned about their methodology and standards.

Teacher performance was evaluated, in part, by having the average number of students get average grades in class: As long as one's grade book looked like a bell curve, without too many As or too many failures, a teacher could expect to work unbothered by poor evaluations. To simplify matters for everyone, a strict mathematical formula for grading students was devised that persists, largely unquestioned and untweaked, to this day.

In many classrooms, for reasons a teacher may find himself or herself unable to explain, 90% is an "A," or an exemplary performance. Students with less than 60% have "earned" a "F," indicating failure. This serves the needs of a large system to run efficiently, but does it communicate whether learning occurred? Why is 90% considered "exemplary"? There are many examples of professions where 90% success would be considered a remarkable and rare feat, for example, in sales. Likewise, there are examples of professions where 90% would be considered absolutely unacceptable, such as in building construction. It is remarkable, and probably wrongheaded, that such amazing consistency would exist across all subjects and ages in schools.

These arbitrary and antiquated grade-distribution practices are not just limited to classrooms. School districts and even state departments of education administer standardized tests and take great pains to carefully examine the results before they are released. These tests have numerical scores attached to them, representing the number of points a student could earn. A recent test in Ohio featured 38 questions and was worth 700 points; however, a judgment on the score came from the state, who determined what is called a "scaled score."

Here is what happened with that student's "raw score." A panel examined the results of all the students statewide and compared the results against a standard bell curve. With this information about the scores, they determined—*after* the test had been administered and scored—whether a given score proved that a student was "limited" or "proficient," or perhaps "advanced."

What these legislators have done is taken a test they claim is truly an assessment of what a student can and can't do, and compared it to a theoretical model. Then they have manipulated the results to fit their preconceived definition of what the results should be. Worse yet, they applied the bell curve, a theory of achievement that has been debunked for being racist, in addition to being bad math.[1]

They have "normed" a standardized test.

Still, other flawed practices and beliefs persist based on these past models of teaching.

In the traditional model of instruction, it was the teacher's job to offer criticism and corrections to each student; exposing mistakes was the primary mode of discourse. How to respond to student mistakes was a question left to be answered solely by the teacher, and answers varied as widely as individual personalities and personal experiences in classrooms. By and large, teachers emulated their own parents' style of verbal corrections and the grading practices of their favorite teachers from past personal experience.

Teachers marked errors in red ink, as their own errors had been marked. They entered the score in the grade book, checked it against the inherited grade scale, wrote a letter score at the top of the page, and moved on to the next task.

The effect on learners was palpable. This approach left generations of students feeling isolated and ineffective or ridiculed. Even today, many adults even express a dislike for school and specific teachers, and almost all of them can relate one or more incidents where students were faulted, criticized, or even insulted by a teacher for not having grasped a concept.

Think about that. Many individuals can relate stories about "teachers" they encountered who publicly poked fun at students for making mistakes in class or practice. They laughed about, or at, a student essentially for not knowing something—the very condition that *must* exist prior to learning something new. How must these individuals think of themselves as teachers, if they can only teach students who already know the matter at hand?

The current "factory model" of instruction and homework is almost absurd on its face. A child is introduced to a new skill in class and given the chance to practice it. She then takes home a set of problems to practice that skill, handing it in the next day. Her score on this is recorded as part of her permanent grade. She then practices the next day and receives similar work the following night, with this—presumably higher—score being averaged in to her overall score.

But is her ability at this point really the *average* of her earlier level and her current level? Is it even actually at the level she scores on a final examination? Probably not. Such factors as fatigue, a failure to understand the instructions, and family disruptions can impact homework scores. Likewise, even "standardized" tests are impacted by subtle but important differences. Nerves, the number of versions of the question available on the test, and even the wording of the questions can contribute to scores that do not necessarily reveal a student's true level of understanding.

Proficiency with a particular concept is rarely measured on a multiple-choice test in the world beyond school. Some teachers offer the argument that grades serve as the primary motivation for students. A casual glance at any typical classroom would reveal that it is not intrinsic in human nature to want to work to improve a midterm grade on a school report card.

Nancy Flanagan, a writer and consultant at *Education Week*, states the problem well in her article "Grading as an Opportunity to Encourage Students" (emphasis hers):

> You'd like to think that a low grade would be construed as a warning, a spur toward greater effort and focus. You'd like to think that—but not so much, at least for some kids. For them, a low grade feels like proof there's no reason to even try.
>
> How do you reconcile that with points gained, percentages achieved, assignments completed and comparatively evaluated—the traditional tools of grading? There's no such thing as a completely objective grade. *Compiling, weighting, and averaging numbers often leaves a good teacher with a grade that doesn't reflect what he understands about the child in question—what that child actually knows and can do.*[2]

"First, do no harm," becomes the directive to those of us doing academic grading. But here is the call to understand the individual student. Flanagan notes that her statement is true "for some kids." This implies, accurately, that there are some students who see poor grades as motivational, just as there are some students who see them as defeating.

THE RESEARCH

Prior to 1950, the U.S. high school graduation rate was less than 60%.[3] Recently, there have been noticeable improvements in the graduation rate, including a 25% reduction of dropouts between 2008 and 2012. The overall graduation rate has increased to more than 80%. The numbers sound good in aggregate; however, as recently as 2012, there were still about 7,000 children a day dropping out of school and/or falling out of their on-time graduation cadre.[4] This is evidence of improvement but still not evidence of widespread satisfaction with school.

Mortimer Adler, father of the Paideia philosophy of education (a classically based educational approach) proclaimed, "The clearer and higher the expectations, the better the results." Some may worry that a call for changes in the grading system, greater academic respect, and success for all students is a repudiation of this philosophy, but the opposite is true. Clear, high standards should be the basis for everything that happens in the classroom. Students who fall short of the highest standards are not to be discouraged or failed, but instead encouraged and supported in persisting until they master the concept. Achieving passing grades for all students is not a surrender. Instead, it's a victory for education.

Psychologist Lev Vygotsky proposed the importance of scaffolding and labeled this area where a student gains skills as the zone of proximal development. He presented this visually as a set of concentric circles, with what a student knows at the center, a slightly larger circle to show what the student is learning, and finally a larger circle of information and skills outside the student's current awareness (see Figure 2.1). This zone identifies the oval where the student needs support to accomplish tasks as the area where learning occurs.

Teachers know that students arrive in classrooms with a range of competencies. A combination of factors and experiences creates much-appreciated diversity. Rigor, in one sense, becomes relative to the individual student. The

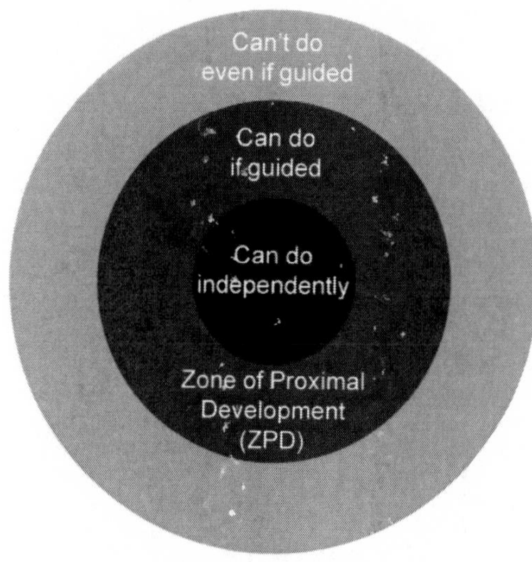

FIGURE 2.1
Zone of Proximal Development

student who lacks factual understanding of a subject must first master the facts, whereas the student with factual understanding must learn to apply that to a real-world scenario to find real rigor. In this way, rigor is dependent on not only the assignment, but also the student's current level of understanding.

To provide appropriate levels of rigor for a wide range of students, resources like Norman L. Webb's Depth of Knowledge (DoK)[5] are important. Webb's DoK "categorizes tasks according to the complexity of thinking required to successfully complete them."[6] This resource provides ways for students to better demonstrate their level of understanding of a concept. The DoK is not a continuum, nor is it sequential or even developmental. Instead, it is a way to understand the complexity of a task and a student's understanding of a concept.

Figure 2.2 is a helpful way to conceive of various facets of rigor in the classroom. Webb's DoK questions help teachers vary the rigor of assignments. Often envisioned as a road map to creating greater rigor, it is especially useful for modifying the level of questions to accommodate the needs of learners at various levels in the same classroom. All levels should be present at various times during instruction or while students are completing assignments, but where students are working more in levels three and four, the teacher will find greater understanding, quicker growth, and more rigor.

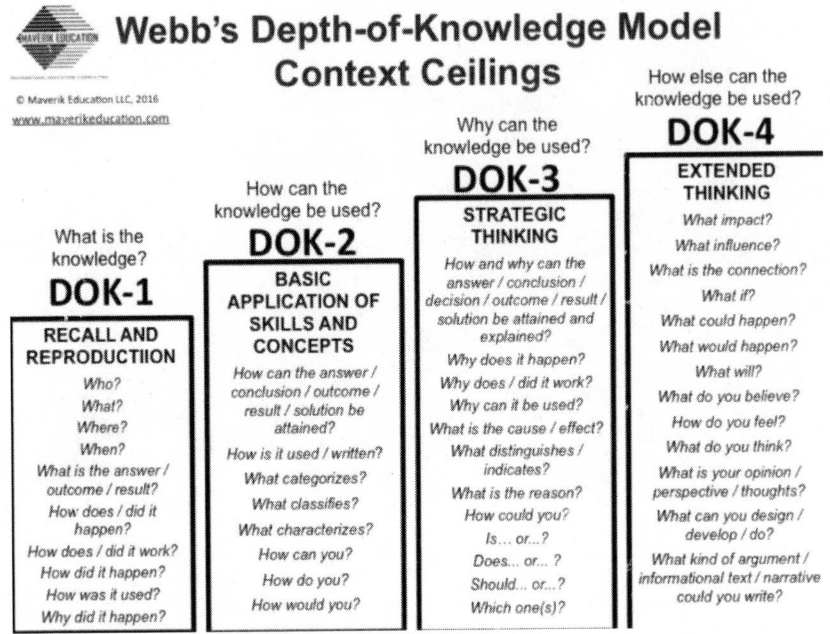

FIGURE 2.2
Webb's Depth of Knowledge. *Maverik Education, www.maverikeducation.com*

SOLUTIONS

Imagine being able to create the following types of conditions in your own classroom: that delicious moment when the bell rings and students moan, "Already?"; students carefully reading the teacher's notes on a homework assignment and placing it in a folder of work to study before the next project; several hands going up each time the teacher asks a question; or students raising their hands again, even immediately after getting a question wrong.

It is possible to construct this classroom, one where respect for the student is the starting point, not a final objective or outcome. This goes beyond merely being polite to students and even beyond cultural understanding—although these are crucial initial principles. This means building systems that are inherently fair and appropriate for each individual student.

These students also need to see a meaningful connection between the work they do and the grades they receive. This relevance is an important part of the relationship between a student and how she feels about the classroom. If a grade simply seems to fall from "on high" without an indication of how it can guide them in improving their skills, students will either accept it if it fits their own self-image or reject it (that is, students who see themselves as good students will accept good grades and reject bad ones). Students with a low self-image will do the opposite.

Important variables that are largely in the teacher's control in the classroom are how time is used, grading practices, authenticity and rigor, and responses to right and wrong answers. How a teacher manages these can have a significant impact on honoring and growing the students in the classroom.

Several years ago, a small delegation of teachers and administrators visited an elementary school to attend a meeting. They were surprised to hear a student being called to the office via the PA system. One teacher wondered aloud whether some personal tragedy or special circumstance had occurred for that student. A few minutes later, a second announcement followed, calling a second student to the office. And then a third. With each interruption to the meeting, the group realized that at that school, it was common to interrupt the learning of every student to take care of the business of the office. How disruptive this must have been in the classroom.

It escapes the ability of science to quantify how this interfered with the act of concentration for the students and staff in the entire school. How many students in a given day must have been on the verge of understanding a concept or grasping a new idea, only to be interrupted by an announcement to summon a student? And the only apparent gain was to make the lives of the office workers simpler, suggesting that the work of the office was more important than the work of the child in the school.

One teacher vowed aloud that this inversion of priorities would never happen at his school, if one day he were to be a principal.

Toward Better Use of Time

Time is the most powerful variable in the classroom and education. But bells ring. There are holidays. Students are sometimes absent. Sure, time is limited in some ways, but this only heightens the importance of how educators use time in the classroom.

In his book *Outliers*, Malcolm Gladwell outlines a common factor among leading innovators, athletes, and experts in a variety of fields—10,000 hours of focused practice. This research reinforced and depended on, in no small amount, the work of Anders Ericsson, a brain scientist whose research suggests the same correlation between practice time and success. While not simple, the number at least seems straightforward. It is measurable, more like a goal than a mystery.

The typical classroom does not offer a student, say, 10,000 hours to master geography; however, the imperative to protect time is real. So how does one protect student time? It should be treated like the most precious commodity available to a teacher, because it is.

One place that teachers can lose or gain time is in transitions. These minutes when class is starting or ending are hidden time vampires, sucking away one to three minutes at the start and end of each bell. Moving between classes takes four to six minutes, depending on the size of the school, and having everyone moving at once makes these transitions slower than they might otherwise be.

The cumulative effect of simply unpacking at the beginning of class and packing up at the end can equate to more than 15 hours of lost instructional time per class during the course of a typical school year. Those 15 hours represent more than three weeks of instruction in a typical high school schedule. Some schools have adopted block schedules to recapture some of that time and reduce interruptions in the classroom.

A teacher does not have to change the entire bell schedule to make the most of class time. Carefully teaching and structuring arrival and departure practices can save this time. When students arrive, do they know what tools they need to have ready to be successful? Do they know what work they can get started on without receiving additional instruction from the teacher? At the end of class, are there clear signals for moving into transition?

One teacher helped manage the end-of-day transition by turning on music to signal end-of-the-day cleanup. Students could hear the music; Michael

Jackson's "Man in the Mirror" was selected to reinforce a theme of taking personal responsibility for one's world. When students heard this music, they knew that it was time to begin the process of winding down the day. They could then quietly pack up and begin their assigned tasks in the classroom, whether cleaning up or preparing items for the next day.

Additionally, capturing this time allows for collaboration and project work. Students in this protected academic environment have time for deep engagement and several modes of learning, including time for mini-lessons, project work, deep involvement in reading a book or article, or getting lost entirely in the act of creation of a work of art or music. Having this time available in this way is a necessary component of "flow," the optimal zone for encouraging repeated practice and growth.

There will always be times when the best solution to a problem is a teacher lecture. This is a powerful tool in the classroom. But many teachers spend too much time in the mode of giving instruction or, worse, feeling as if they need to entertain the class. In the class, time can also be captured by making sure that instruction is differentiated or otherwise tailored to the individual needs of students.

Students learn best in an environment where they are being challenged just at or beyond their level of current skill. Working in their zone of proximal development, described earlier, means they are getting the most growth out of each available minute in the classroom. Providing work in this zone for students increases their chances of experiencing deep concentration.

The research of Mihaly Csikszentmihalyi revealed that individual engagement and interest peak when the demands of the task were closely related to the individual's skill level. In *The Conditions of Flow*, Csikszentmihalyi outlines how athletes and musicians are able to "flow" for long periods of time—that is, in working constantly to get better and match their level of struggle with their level of ability, they grow more skillful and lose track of the passage of time.[7] This is his description of a feeling everyone has when they are genuinely engaged in learning, and this is considered by many to be evidence of peak human experience.

This happens for people in academic settings, too. Writing, reading, exploring a model, researching, or working on a project can induce this same experience of timeless, deep concentration. For teachers, the act of protecting periods of uninterrupted time where students have autonomy over the choice of work in the classroom allows flow to happen more often. This is what sets up those moments when the bell rings and the students ask, "Already?!"

The use of questions to develop the deep practice of specialized, broken-down skills actually changes the chemistry of the brain. Science has revealed that the act of thinking involves sending electrical impulses through the brain's circuitry. As pathways are used again and again, myelin—a coating on neural pathways—forms, making the pathways more durable and helping the brain function more efficiently. Reviewing newly formed connections helps develop myelin in the brain. This is especially helpful in recalling important information and mastering key skills.

The effective use of time and practice is how a student becomes a master of anything. Thus, in addition to capturing time for the group, it is important to work to capture individual attention and time through any means possible. For instance, if a teacher can use guided practice and questioning to challenge an entire classroom in answering a question instead of one student at a time, it dramatically increases the overall academic growth and engagement time.

If a teacher can tailor the practice to a specific skill, perhaps using the correct conjugation of verbs in Spanish, and cram in a dozen practices of the skill where there used to be only one or two, this is making student growth a factor in the traditional classroom. That's a lot of myelin, laying the groundwork for a superhighway of correct skills.

One way to capture this time is by using the teacher habit known as "no opt out," discussed in Doug Lemov's book *Teach Like a Champion*.[8] This habit not only captures time, but also increases engagement in the classroom, while providing extra repetitions for students. The concept is simple and starts out like in a typical classroom.

The first iteration of "no opt out" comes from the expectation that every student should be able to answer every question, or at least try to answer it. One cannot "opt out" of their education. During lecture, or any other time when a teacher is reviewing work with one or more students, the teacher asks questions. If a student does not answer, he is misbehaving, and the teacher will quickly circle back. If a student gives an incorrect or incomplete answer, the teacher asks another student to complete the answer or the teacher provides it.

Then comes the "no opt out": The teacher turns and asks the question again to the student who either did not answer or provided an incorrect or incomplete answer. The student then must give the correct or complete answer.

In a traditional classroom questioning model, this student would have tuned out after getting the wrong answer and, in fact, only had practice reciting the *wrong* answer. The traditional approach wastes classroom time and reinforces the wrong answer.

With "no opt out," each student is responsible for listening carefully to the correction and reproducing the correct answer. This gives the student (and everyone else in the class) additional practice with the correct answer. When coupled with the practice of "cold call"—calling on students seemingly randomly throughout the lesson—this creates a powerful incentive for students to pay attention throughout the lesson and be responsible for getting the answer fully correct. Now the time that used to be used for one student to do the thinking is used by the entire class—25 students thinking instead of one.

Toward Better Grading Practices

Earlier, Nancy Flanagan pointed out that traditional grading is often not objective and frequently saps a student's willingness to try harder. But evaluation and feedback could be used to do so much more than determining a student's final grade in a class. Teachers must work to understand each child's relationship with grading—what will spur greater effort?

Teachers can learn this by asking students about their past grades and what that shows about them, perhaps with a simple survey.

> Tell me about a grade you got in the past that you are proud of.
>
> Tell me about a grade in the past that made you frustrated.
>
> What, if anything, do your past grades reveal about you?
>
> Remember an assignment you were proud of. What made you proud about it?

With one or more of these questions, which could be asked at the start of the year when discussing past classes or in the middle of the year when talking about one's own class, a teacher can get a sense of the student's feelings about grading and whether these grades and the current grading practices are motivational or defeating. It is when the teacher knows the student well that progress can truly be evaluated.

Barb Scholtz, the practicum director at CMStep, an international secondary Montessori teacher and administrator education program, asks a simple question about this use of grades: If a child is learning, how can they be failing? That question is fair, and it is devastating to the traditional system of student evaluation. Thus, if teachers are to adhere to the concept of first doing no harm, we must escape the conviction that bad grades will motivate a student.

Alfie Kohn has written extensively about grading and pointed out the wrongheaded thinking about how grades motivate. In an article entitled "Grading," published on his website, he challenges the common concept that bad grades are motivational:

> The trouble lies with the implicit assumption that there exists a single entity called "motivation" that students have to a greater or lesser degree. In reality, a critical and qualitative difference exists between intrinsic and extrinsic motivation—between an interest in what one is learning for its own sake and a mindset in which learning is viewed as a means to an end, the end being to escape a punishment or snag a reward. Not only are these two orientations distinct, but they also often pull in opposite directions.[9]

Kohn advocates for an approach that is starting to seem less radical as teachers seek to teach for mastery. He calls for ending traditional grading altogether. Eliminating grades and replacing them with a standards-based or mastery-based system creates positive feelings about the class.[10] This is not a surprise; the root of this feeling could be discovered in our own humanity. Humans wish to be engaged and involved in constructing the systems around us.

Instead, comments meant to challenge the student to further delve into what they are learning and an expectation that changes will be made to present the best possible final work are the best possible motivators for students. This also means that teachers must stand firm against the idea that missed work should be punished with a "0" and then the student should move on to the next assignment.

It is hard to imagine a world-of-work scenario where the entire project is predicated on the timeliness of the work. Does a construction team walk away from an unfinished hotel? Would one want the car repair shop to simply walk away from a brake job at the moment the deadline arrives? If an IEP falls past a deadline, does the interventionist simply drop the work and move on to other things? No, no, and no.

The origins of the "take the 0" arose when the purpose of school was to separate the college-bound from the factory-bound. Using time as a factor in evaluating students was a good way to "grade" students, in the traditional sense of making distinctions between students in as many ways as possible. If they did not get the work done in time, they got a poor grade.

This is an impractical approach if the work of teaching is truly to get everyone to master the same material. Time is a variable, in today's schools. It is not an indicator of student capacity for understanding or even whether the work got done.

If the work assigned by teachers in the classroom is truly valuable, teachers must treat it that way. A teacher cannot tell a student on Tuesday that the work is crucial and then tell him on Friday to take the "0" and move on.

Aaron was a young teacher quickly growing proficient at his craft, but he was struggling with the challenges of finding the fairest grading practices in his room. He approached his principal with a series of questions. Through the questions and answers, they came to realize they were discussing ways to use grades to increase student motivation.

Aaron was unhappy with the number of students who did not complete the homework and, consequently, were failing his class. He was looking for possible solutions.

His principal selected a sports metaphor from an article he had read years before. The article had asked, essentially, "What if grading at school was more like sports?" Their conversation went something like this:

Principal: Where do you get graded in football?

Aaron: On the scoreboard Friday night.

Principal: And if you mess up at practice?

Aaron: You practice it again. (*Shrugging*) And maybe get yelled at.

Principal: I'm not a fan of yelling in the classroom.

Aaron: It would get things going, though.

The principal understood that Aaron was not really a yeller but that he was just playing devil's advocate.

Principal: (*Shaking his head and uttering*) Just, no.

Aaron: (*Shaking his head*) Can I make them do wind sprints? How about push-ups?

Principal: Really, you just keep practicing, right? And how do you get graded Sunday afternoon?

Aaron: The score. The score is your grade. It is real, it counts.

Principal: So, what was it you did all week? Does it count? Like, if you practice hard, do you get extra points?

Aaron: No, you just improve your chances of getting extra points.

Principal: And if you don't practice?

Aaron: Well, you play terribly.

Principal: Yes, but I don't know a coach who lets you play if you didn't practice.

Aaron: Fair point.

The result of the conversation between Aaron and his principal was a somewhat research-based and somewhat metaphorically bound new grading policy. Students had to practice to play. That is, they had to complete the required classwork and homework to take the quizzes or complete the projects that would determine their final grade. Students who are not done practicing are not yet ready to "play."

This new policy included the provision that a student could not even sit for a summative test until he had completed the reading and preparation covered on the test. There was no more insistence to "just take the 0." Of course, this policy works best when those students who require additional support are given the time they need to prepare.

Aaron and the principal ran into a common obstacle to classroom innovation: a parent who was more comfortable with the traditional approach.

Aaron and the principal reported this anecdote about the policy change: During the first week of implementation, a longtime parent and one of the school's biggest supporters was upset when her son could not take an exam. The parent had experienced a traditional system and insisted that her son be allowed to take the zero on his homework and proceed to take the test. She was unsatisfied after talking with Aaron, and her next call was to the principal.

Fortunately, her son and husband were athletes, so when the principal provided the rationale, which relied heavily on the sports comparison, the parent relented a bit. Once she came to understand that the teacher was giving extended time and there were multiple chances for her son to take the test after he completed the "practice," she agreed to give the policy a chance.

When her son completed the work, a couple of weeks after the original due date, he sat for the test during lunchtime. He did well: His grade on the test was better than his typical social studies score. He and his mother attributed the improved score to the fact that he had completed the work. He played better because he had practiced, and both mother and father became supporters of the policy.

Toward Authentic Instruction and Grading

A student's score on a given assignment can fluctuate widely based on a range of factors, including homework environment, ability to understand how a question is phrased, and attention to detail. Our final system of evaluating students' achievement should acknowledge this and factor in progress toward a goal as part of the final grade. This can include, but should not depend on, a strict average of the scores on completed work.

A better way is to provide authentic assessment. At Paula's school, students complete a yearlong project during their senior year. The final product is included in a showcase during the last week of school that is open to the public. Students invite family members and their topic mentor, and the school's doors are open to the public. Members of the public are invited to provide feedback on the students' work, including positive comments and questions they still have about the research or presentation.

Perhaps more than any other assessment during their high school career, students are anxious and excited about these presentations. They spend days working together, thinking about how to organize their presentation boards and arrange their artifacts on the table. When they are finished, they hug one another in relief and celebration, laughing and talking as they help one another dismantle their displays.

This is the kind of excitement that mimics real-world work and presentations. The project involves meaningful deadlines, real audiences, and experts helping to assess the work. It is not practical to think that every assignment can be this way; however, it is not fair to students if they have no assignments like this during the course of the year.

In the opening anecdote of this chapter, a six-year-old boy displays an immense specialized vocabulary relative to the card game Pokémon, which captures his imagination. This yearning to understand exactly what something is called and use this new vocabulary in a specialized way is an innate human characteristic. Every teacher has seen similar levels of mastery in her students, although unfortunately it is seldom exhibited toward the subject taught by the teacher. Perhaps this is not the student's fault.

How often have teachers, in a hurry to move on to the next aspect of the lesson, accepted language that was shorthand for the intended term? How often have teachers allowed precision in language to diminish in the classroom?

Adults watching the game show *Are You Smarter Than a Fifth Grader?* often find themselves musing, "I used to know that," as questions come up about legal procedures and grammar. How is it that people once knew these things and now they do not? The answer is lack of practice and lack of relevance.

Teachers sometimes tend to move away from precise language, hoping to create greater engagement, when, in fact, students are tuning out. Teachers must continue to use technical terms and professional examples in the classroom, refining and enhancing the use of exact vocabulary for concepts covered in class. Doing anything less diminishes students' interests and passions, and retards their learning.

This relates to an additional important classroom habit prescribed in *Teach Like a Champion*, which Lemov calls "format matters." This is a teacher habit of requiring students to always give an answer in a professionally acceptable and accurate format. For example, a science teacher asking a student the volume of a sphere with a radius of one meter would not accept "4.19" as an answer. This teacher would prompt, "Format?" And the student would revise her answer to "4.19 meters cubed." The human mind craves this level of precision, and demanding it causes greater student interest and involvement.

Toward the Right Response to Wrong Answers

When a student gives a wrong or incomplete answer, even one that seems unrelated to the topic at hand, the teacher's job is to *not* immediately provide the correct answer—at least not all the time. Instead, there are a range of strategies the teacher should employ.

First, ask a question that elicits a defense of the answer. How did you get this answer? Why do you think that? These questions can help the teacher get to what he needs to hear. The student response can show a connection that is not readily apparent to the teacher. Or, more often, it can show a misunderstanding of a key concept or term that will unlock real understanding.

Many student errors are predictable to the experienced teacher. Asking about the thought process speeds up identification of the misconception and allows the teacher to quickly diagnose the problem and provide appropriate intervention. Math students often miss a symbol indicating, perhaps, that a number is negative or that a parenthetical expression was to be completed first. Allowing students to strengthen the connection between what they thought was true and what they are learning pays everlasting dividends. It also shows respect for the thinking process.

Another option is to open up the question to other students to provide a correct answer. Then, for greater sophistication, ask classmates or the student herself to identify the mistake made. One teacher peppered his classroom rapport with terms of endearment for student errors: "Excellent mistake," or "Oh, great wrong answer!" or "I love that mistake." Or "Can anyone see why this is a mistake, and why I love it?" What would follow was a brief conversation with students where they pointed out common mistakes in thinking that came from not understanding a process or a lack of careful reading.

Moreover, this modeling was important for a student who felt the work was not worthwhile or too hard. He saw his peers pointing out that they understood something and reviewing the pathway to that way of thinking. This is peer "pressure" being put to positive use. For some students, the urge to demonstrate that they understand something a classmate does not can be inspirational, and it gives more and more students a chance to be producers rather than receivers of knowledge.

When a student gives an incorrect answer, sometimes the mistake is a lack of completeness. Here, the teacher can encourage with a word or two: "Say more" or "What do you mean?" This forces students to review their own thinking or flesh it out a bit more. In one class, a student stood to approach the teacher's desk with a question. He was clearly working out how to ask the question. Midway through, he stopped and said, "Oh!" He returned to his seat. The simple act of trying to form the question caused additional thinking and, ultimately, an insight that was only possible in the classroom.

Another option is to provide the correct answer, with a follow-up question. For example, "Nope, that was an example of asexual reproduction. Can you see the key piece of information that you missed?" Driving students back to their answers and thinking is key. Students who come to see errors as normal in the classroom become less resistant to correction in general.

Praise what is right in the answer, even if this means seeing that the student was trying to take the right step but failed. Make a connection to an earlier or less sophisticated understanding of the topic at hand. Then follow up with a prompt to a deeper understanding.

It is important to use language that helps couch the mistake in the learning process, rather than indicate a student's ability level. It is also important to use these same terms and strategies when students give correct answers.

Importantly, a teacher should not always telegraph via their response whether the answer is correct. A teacher can really get a class thinking when, following a correct answer, she asks the class, "How did you get this answer?" It is especially powerful if students have become accustomed to hearing this as a response to an incorrect answer. Enlisting students to think about the answer even deeper, in the hopes of figuring out why it might be wrong or incomplete, develops deeper thinking and creates the habit of rigorous self-correction and clarification.

Normalizing mistakes and returning with the "no opt out" practice to emphasize the learning process builds habits of mind and structure in the classroom. This allows for repeated, targeted practice and the best use of time for students.

CONCLUSION

Aside from expressing concern for students as individuals, there are dozens of ways for a teacher to demonstrate respect for students as learners within each lesson. The teacher is responsible for creating and demonstrating respect for students by providing a structure in the classroom that fosters intellectual curiosity and comfort, where making mistakes is part of learning.

For far too long, teachers have treated time as a set metric, while squandering vast amounts of it in the classroom each day. For too long, teachers have allowed the learning of an entire class to come to a halt as one student struggles to provide an answer, only to offer a feeble "I don't know" and have the conversation keep moving right along. For too long, students have seen wrong answers as fatal flaws to be avoided, especially in front of their peers. And for too long, grades and other feedback have been perceived as immutable judgments on students' intelligence, rather than a means to work harder and improve skills.

In a nurturing classroom, educators can take each of these items, previously unexamined and unquestioned, and leverage them to create greater involvement and growth. Students who might not have previously had a voice can now feel free to take chances and speak out. Papers that once got shoved into the bottom of book bags and thrown away during winter break can now provide insight and guidance for the next major assignment.

TIPS OF THE TRADE

- Question everything in your classroom.
- Manage time carefully.
    - Capture time by creating efficient practices at the start and end of class.
    - Capture time by using "no opt out" and "cold call" to keep students engaged and producing correct answers throughout the lesson.

- Review your grading policy to ensure that it offers opportunities for measuring student growth, not just recording scores; avoids penalizing students for poor practice on a new concept; and requires completing practice work.
- Provide authentic work and assessments.
    - Structure meaningful, standards-based work.
    - Increase the rigor of practice by requiring students to respond with technically accurate language.
    - Offer authentic assessment of work by inviting the public to review assignments.
    - Review your assignments to see where they fall on Webb's DoK chart.
- Respond to right and wrong answers in similar ways.
    - Ask for clarification of the answer.
    - Request more information about how the answer was derived.
    - Ask classmates to evaluate the answer.
- Know where individual students are relative to the standards and provide differentiated work to meet their needs (see chapter 6) in their zone of proximal development.

3

Building a Caring and Supportive Community in the Classroom and Beyond

December 15, 2008. That date mournfully remained on the classroom chalkboard for days. No one wanted to erase it. No one wanted to update it.

Changing the date every morning was Cassie's classroom job, and on that date, Cassie's mother had died unexpectedly. Cassie hadn't returned to school yet, and the students wanted to honor her absence and the tragic loss that she had experienced by leaving the date just as it was the last time she was present to change it.

In this classroom, a loss experienced by any student was a loss to everyone because they were connected to one another—they were an interdependent community. Without Cassie present, they were less than whole, and they didn't want to resume as if things were normal until she was able to be with them again.

A crucial component to any school's success is the intentional development and fostering of a sense of community—also referenced as "school connectedness" or a "sense of belonging." Humans crave interpersonal engagement and the feeling that they are a part of a group. Adolescents have a particularly powerful need for this as they wrestle with straddling the divide between childhood and adulthood, and push for greater independence from parents and other family members.

Schools are in a unique position to be able to consciously create a structure to fulfill this need. Students attend school with similarly aged peers for 6 or more hours each day, 5 days a week, for 13 years. Schools must maximize this opportunity to create a place in which students feel inherently connected, a place where they belong.

THE PROBLEM

Much has been written and discussed during the past few years about the state of American education; however, little of this discourse has included concerns about building a sense of school connectedness. In fact, as a result of the school reform movement, which is heavily laden with standardized testing requirements and school accountability regulations, a student's feelings of belonging at school may, in fact, be decreasing even further. Certainly, teachers and administrators feel pressured to reduce, or even eliminate, any instructional time that is spent on anything outside the bounds of curricular content.

On its surface, this singular focus on academic instruction may seem intuitive—if improved academic outcomes are needed, spend more time on academic instruction. But that understanding is misguided, because until students feel like they belong at school, like they are a part of something bigger than themselves, the time spent on content may be lost. As Maslow noted, until basic needs, like that of belonging, are met, humans are unable to work toward the achievement of higher-level needs.

Adolescents spend more time at school than they spend engaged in any other single activity.[1] Developing a sense of community at school, also referenced as "school connectedness," is crucial for students; however, it is an area where schools tend to struggle. About half of secondary students (40 to 60%) report being disconnected from school.[2] Based on survey data, schools with a strong sense of community are rare.[3]

The typical U.S. high school is structured around a seemingly factory-style model. Large numbers of students are enrolled in a building, and students spend each day assigned to six or seven class bells, each with a different teacher and a different group of peers. There is little time given to the intentional establishment of community, and, generally, the activities provided occur just a few times each year and take the form of pep rallies or assemblies.

This traditional approach leaves students to independently fill their basic human need for belonging and connection through peer relationships—at best, this is simply not enough to create strong school communities, and at worst, it can be damaging and even downright dangerous. Making unsafe decisions as a result of peer pressure is an attempt to fill a need to belong. The formation and joining of gangs is an extreme form of fulfilling this intrinsic need.

Adolescents crave belonging. That's why they are so drawn to powerful peer groups, clubs, teams, gangs, and other quasi-organized social groupings. It is also why Cassie's peers refused to change the date on the board until she returned to take her rightful role in the classroom.

THE RESEARCH

It is especially important that adolescents are provided with healthy ways to fulfill their need to belong. Seventy-five percent of deaths of people ages 11 to 20 are caused by unintentional injuries, homicide, and suicide.[4] Additionally, adolescents are at risk for engaging in other types of dangerous behaviors. Examples include substance use (cigarettes, alcohol, and drugs); such violent behaviors as the possession of weapons; and early or unprotected sexual activity, leading to increased risk of teen pregnancy and sexually transmitted diseases.

Feeling connected to a school community has been linked to the reduced likelihood that students will engage in violent or delinquent behavior, drink alcohol, use drugs, or engage in early sexual activity. Moreover, students who report high levels of school connectedness indicate lower levels of physical and emotional distress and fewer symptoms of depression, and they are less likely to engage in suicidal ideation or suicide attempts. Better academic outcomes are also noted for students who indicate that they feel connected to their school community.

The relationship between a sense of belonging at school and improved behavioral and academic outcomes appears to be both bidirectional and causal.[5]

In other words, while feelings of school connectedness are protective for students, feelings of being disconnected from school increase risky behaviors and decrease academic performance.

Furthermore, increasing feelings of school connection have a positive effect on behavioral and academic performance, while decreasing feelings of connection at school have a similar negative effect. This powerful data is consistent across gender and ethnicity, and similar results have been documented internationally.[6]

With such powerful benefits when it is present and such deleterious impacts in its absence, school connectivity is something that must be given attention and intentionally fostered. The consequences are simply too great to ignore this issue. But how can teachers and administrators move away from the previously described "factory-style" model of education and toward a school structure that supports the development of school community?

All great schools have stories that demonstrate the many ways in which students and staff perpetuate and promote school connectedness, but what are the reproducible elements that create this?

THE SOLUTION

Four specific practices have been identified as being most crucial to developing community in schools:

1. Emphasizing common purposes and ideals.
2. Cultivating respectful, supportive relationships among students, teachers, and parents.
3. Offering regular occasions for service and cooperation.
4. Providing developmentally appropriate opportunities for autonomy and influence.

Emphasizing Common Purposes and Ideals

When students and staff throughout a program maintain the same values, expectations, and procedures, students have clarity in what is expected of them, and they can work toward upholding those same expectations throughout the course of their education. This helps them feel as if they are part of something greater than a classroom group, or even a grade-level group; they are part of the school community, and this is "what we do here."

Those words, and the idea that there is a code of ethics that defines a program, help students to identify themselves with the positive behavioral expectations that have been established. Maya's story is a powerful example of the establishment of a code of conduct that becomes "what we do here" in a way that clearly demonstrates the impact of this concept.

When Maya arrived in seventh grade, she had some behavioral concerns. She didn't hesitate to engage in conflict and was unwilling to back down to avoid a physical altercation. Throughout the course of several years, she connected with adults and peers, learned strategies for self-control, and began to emerge as a positive role model for others.

During the first week of school of her sophomore year, a student new to the building challenged Maya, leading to a verbal altercation. When the other student, without warning, hauled off and hit Maya square in the face, Maya looked up, startled, and said, "Somebody's gotta tell her that's not what we do here."

"That's not what we do here." The idea that we are part of a community that maintains a code of ethics that we inspire one another to achieve is powerful. That *is* what we do here, and anything outside of those guidelines is *not* what we do here. Maya knew this, and understanding it so deeply allowed her to choose a different and far more proactive approach than she would have been capable of three years earlier.

Cultivating Respectful, Supportive Relationships

Schools and classrooms can be purposefully structured to allow for the development of positive relationships between peers and teachers and students. There are tremendous benefits for students through the implementation of a team-based model of education. While team-based schools are few and far between, they are powerful resources for developing community, and it is a model that is growing in popularity.

At Gamble Montessori, as with other team-based programs, when students arrive at Gamble in the seventh grade, they are assigned to one of four communities. Each community is comprised of 50 to 60 seventh and eighth grade students and three teachers—a math/science teacher, a language arts/social studies teacher, and an intervention specialist (special educator).

Students stay in this community for both years of junior high, and they receive core curriculum instruction with the same teachers and students. This allows students and teachers to form powerful bonds. Rather than a teacher seeing six bells of 30 students each, for a total of 180 students each day, and 360 students during the course of a two-year period, teachers work with an average of only 55 students each day and 84 students in a two-year cycle. Thus, they have the ability to develop a personal relationship with each student.

In addition, in a traditional secondary school structure, students are enrolled in seven bells of approximately 30 students; therefore, they have the potential of having classes with as many as 200 different peers each day. When students are able to spend the majority of their class time with a consistent group of peers, it makes a tremendous difference in their ability to connect with others at school.

Research indicates that students who have a positive relationship with an adult at school demonstrate greater resiliency in the face of adversity; they are better able to avoid the risk-taking behavior defined previously. A study conducted over a span of 40 years determined that,

> among the most frequently encountered positive role models in the lives of resilient children, outside of the family circle, was a favorite teacher who was not just an instructor for academic skills for the youngsters, but also a confidante and positive model for personal identification. . . . It is obvious that children will work harder to do things . . . for people they love and trust.[7]

"It is obvious that children will work harder to do things for people they love and trust." It is this very thing that we are so at risk of losing. When we overload our classrooms with rigid academic instruction and test preparation at the expense of exploration of interests, creative projects, intentional development of social–emotional learning, and activities that build positive relationships, we are in jeopardy of exorcizing the "love and trust" teachers know is so crucial to learning. Teachers must actively seek strategies to de-

velop relationships with students, even if this comes at the cost of time that might otherwise be used for test preparation.

The important question school personnel must explore is how to know which students are at risk for feeling disconnected. It is all too easy, and too common, to assume that "the kids are alright."

Sometimes the simplest strategy is the best. Instead of assuming that we know which children in our classrooms are not feeling connected, we can just ask them. A basic survey can be used to determine, among other things, which students do not believe they have a supportive adult at school.

At Gamble Montessori, when we implemented a survey, 72% of students indicated at least one staff person with whom they felt a strong sense of connection. Of these, most students listed a number of staff people, and many identified all of the teachers on their teaching team. This not only served as a powerful indicator of the strong work we were doing with building relationships through our team-based model, but also allowed us to clearly identify the 28% of students who felt disconnected and therefore were at risk.

The most important step was to then consciously assign teachers to reach out to those students who did not feel a sense of connection to try and ensure that, ultimately, they did develop feelings of school connectedness.

For example, when Mynasia came to Gamble as a seventh grader, she was quite the rough-and-tumble young lady, but she quickly settled into the expectations of our program and, by the end of that year, had emerged as an all-star student, both academically and in terms of classroom leadership. This was due, in large part, to the relationships she developed with her teachers.

During her eighth grade year, in a casual conversation, she shared information with her teacher, Ms. Donnoly, about significant alcohol use and verbal abuse that were occurring in her home. It was a difficult story to listen to, and by the end of it, Ms. Donnoly knew that as a state-mandated reporter, she was going to have to notify Child Protective Services. This is always a difficult position to be placed in. Rarely does the child want you to make the report, and although these reports are anonymous, they always jeopardize the relationship between school staff and adults in the home.

Mynasia had trusted Ms. Donnoly with the information, and more than anything, Ms. Donnoly did not want to violate that trust. When Ms. Donnoly was ready to make the call, she pulled Mynasia out of class and told her what she had to do and why she had to do it. Mynasia was clearly afraid—afraid of what would happen at home, afraid that she would be removed from her family, afraid of the unknown.

Ms. Donnoly told Mynasia she didn't want there to be any surprises or misunderstandings; she asked Mynasia to be present when she made the report, so she knew exactly what was being said. Together, they sat at a desk, and when Ms. Donnoly had answered all of her questions, she asked Mynasia if she was ready for her to place the call. Mynasia nodded yes and then quietly slipped her hand into Ms. Donnoly's grasp. Ms. Donnoly picked up the phone, dialed the number, and made the report. Throughout the call, she held Mynasia's hand and, at the end, promised she would let her know the outcome as soon as it was shared with her.

Ultimately, the report was filed, but no investigation was opened. Mynasia was relieved, and Ms. Donnoly was confident that she had done the right thing—both in terms of filing the report and the way she cared for Mynasia while doing so. Ms. Donnoly will never forget the power of holding Mynasia's hand during that phone call or the feeling of solidarity this simple action created.

Teacher–Student Relationships

These individual relationships between teachers and students yield both small and large benefits on a near daily basis. There are hundreds, if not thousands, of stories that could be used to illustrate their impact.

Home–School Relationships

Working with a smaller number of students and staying with them for two years helps develop home–school connections with parents as well. All schools hold parent–teacher conferences, but at schools that implement student-led conferences, these meetings look different. Student-led conferences, as stated in their name, are led by the student. It is the student whose performance is being discussed; therefore, the student ought to lead the conversation.

This process allows the child to self-report on how things are going at school and provides the opportunity for the student to take responsibility for both what is going well and what is not. Additionally, when information is shared together and everyone hears the same message at the same time, it creates a sense of collaboration between the student, the parent, and the teacher. It is another component to "what we do here."

However, many urban schools struggle with low levels of parent involvement.[8] It is important to remember that many parents experience anxiety about involvement in their child's school. This may be because of negative school experiences they had themselves, worries that either their child or their parenting skills will be critiqued, or concerns about their ability to understand the academic instruction being provided.

As a teacher, there are strategies to alleviate some of this discomfort, which, in turn, allows the parent or guardian to engage fully with school staff to support the academic and developmental growth of the child.

- Begin each interaction with something positive about the child.
- Do not label a child; rather, describe the behavior you have observed.
  - Instead of "Brad is lazy," say, "Brad is not spending time working on his assignments, and they are not getting completed."
  - Instead of "Suzie is sneaky," say, "Suzie has been copying off other students' work, and she sometimes takes other's belongings."
- Assume the parent or guardian is doing the best that they can; however, do not assume they already know how to address concerns.
  - Provide explicit suggestions for ways they can support the child at home (e.g., check in with a student nightly to review what work needs to be completed, set aside quiet time for study, provide a homework space where supervision can occur).
  - Share ways to cultivate good study habits and techniques for review.
  - Gently offer suggestions for behavior-management strategies if this is a concern.
- Open the door to further communication.
- Remember that you are teaching other people's children, that every student you serve is someone's child—their most precious gift—and they have chosen to share this gift with you.

Parents can be a teacher's greatest ally in working with students. Every interaction a teacher has with students' parents or guardians can serve as an opportunity to strengthen the relationship, even if the conversation is a difficult one.

There are few conversations to have with parents that are more challenging than those that involve significant disciplinary action. When students are assigned to out-of-school consequences—emergency removal from school, suspension, or expulsion—a parent conference is sometimes part of the required process for reentry into the classroom. These discussions can be hard; for the student to have been removed from school, the behavior in question had to be significant.

Sometimes parents are angry with school staff; often they are embarrassed by their child's behavior. Teachers have already had to manage and document the student's misbehavior, and holding the reentry conference requires more of their valuable time and energy. Yet, these conversations can be some of the most powerful talks teachers engage in, due, in large part, to the help of a structured process.

At Gamble Montessori, these meetings open with each person at the table sharing what they perceive as the strengths of the child. Then teachers, parents, and the student each have an opportunity to share concerns. Options for supporting the child are examined through the lenses of what school staff will do, what the parent will do, and what the student will do. All parties involved then sign a form.

This process is far more valuable than the enforcement of the consequence that triggered the conference. The discussion smooths the return of the child to the classroom for everyone and resets the expectation of success and the idea that parents, teachers, and the student are working together to help achieve this goal.

For example, without these types of meetings, it would have been easy for Deon's mother to develop an adversarial relationship with school staff. Deon was a student who struggled tremendously with inappropriate behavior. His teachers were frustrated because he disrupted their classrooms on a near-daily basis.

By the end of the school year, Deon had more than 40 documented disciplinary incidents. We were holding yet another reentry conference for him, and the stage was set for conflict. Deon believed he was being picked on by school staff. He had shared this with his mother, and she, understandably, arrived at the conference prepared to fight for her child.

This scenario would have done nothing to help Deon be more successful; instead, it would have caused him to become even further estranged from his teachers, which would have failed to reduce the significant problems he was creating in the classroom. But beginning the conversation by sharing the strengths of the child works miracles to deescalate a situation.

Deon presented a significant management problem; given the circumstances, it was difficult to like him or find positive things to say about him. It is in these moments that it is most important to remember that every child brings gifts and demonstrates positive character attributes at one time or another. When seeking Deon's strengths, one teacher, Mr. Thompson, remembered a situation that had occurred the previous school year.

It was the last day of school. To celebrate, Mr. Thompson had taken his students outside for a game of kickball. Although this began as great fun, a number of male students quickly became highly competitive, and frustration mounted as one team took a rapid and significant lead. Deon's team was losing and was in the field as the other team scored run after run. Kim, a student with Down syndrome, came up to bat, and Deon was pitching.

Sensing what he believed was about to occur, Mr. Thompson quickly yelled Deon's name to get his attention. Deon ignored his teacher, so Mr. Thompson yelled again. This time, Deon turned and looked at him, and clearly and calmly stated, "Don't worry, Mr. Thompson, I've got this. I know what to do." He then proceeded to roll the ball slowly, directly over the plate, and after Kim kicked it, he fielded it in a manner that ensured she arrived safely at first base.

In that moment, Mr. Thompson saw a different person from the one he typically witnessed in the classroom, and when he shared this story with Deon's mother during his disciplinary conference, she cried. Instead of being someone who was out to get her child, Mr. Thompson suddenly shifted into someone who saw her son the way she saw him. The staff were no longer adversaries, and as Deon's mother clearly stated at the end of the meeting, "We are all on the same team—Team Deon."

Offering Regular Opportunities for Service and Cooperation

You may have heard the saying, "Always leave a place better than you found it." This sentiment, however, is not something that develops intuitively. Students must be instructed in this concept, and time must be built into a classroom routine to allow for it. In some schools, students are expected to restore the classroom space at the conclusion of each bell by collecting their materials, clearing their table, and pushing in their chairs. The last class of each day is tasked with restoring the classroom environment more fully by wiping down tables and countertops, erasing boards, watering plants or caring for classroom pets, returning materials to their correct locations, organizing supplies, sweeping or vacuuming the floor, and preparing the room for the following day. Additional time can be built into the last period of the day to allow for this important work to occur before dismissal. Moreover, at the end of each lunch period, a rotating group of students could wipe down the cafeteria tables and sweep the floor.

Students may question why they are required to do this "additional" work and why this isn't the job of the custodial staff. In most schools, the custodians—or the teachers—would likely be doing these tasks, but it is important for students to have responsibility and caretaking roles for the space they work in each day.

Although certainly there are benefits for the custodial staff, that is not the driving force behind this practice; rather, when students have collaborative ownership of taking care of the building, they are more likely to feel as if they belong to the community. They have an essential role in ensuring that things run smoothly and are cared for. It is not punishment or "extra," it is simply "what we do here."

The philosophy of leaving a place "better than we found it" should extend beyond the walls of the school building as well. When students go out into the real world for field experiences, the expectation of leaving a place better also must be practiced there, so require students to pick up the space prior to departure. On lengthier trips, conduct full cleanings of the space: take out trash, sweep floors, wipe down bathhouses, and even clean Porta-Potties.

This practice will pleasantly surprise your hosting organization. Share their acknowledgments for this work with your students, because it is important for them to feel the impact of their service and the gratitude that it generates. This reinforces the idea that they do not do the work because they have to; they do it because it is a means of contributing cooperatively through service.

Service Learning

Research has demonstrated that participating in community service yields significant gains for students, including higher grade-point averages, higher graduation rates, increased self-esteem, better overall emotional health, the development of career skills, and a lifelong commitment to giving back.

Many schools have embedded a community-service requirement into their program.

The expectation that students participate in service work is broader than the concept of simply "leaving a place better than we found it." The most common model for student service is a service-hours requirement, but this type of program may be less impactful than intended, in part because it is difficult to enforce and monitor, but also because when students are left on their own to complete these required hours outside of the school day, they don't necessarily understand what service is or how to conduct it.

Many hours may be logged in service to families—free babysitting, dog walking, and so forth. While this may be appropriate for a younger student, older students should be expected to engage in more meaningful service work that fulfills a need in the broader community.

The switch to a service-learning model means that students are provided with instruction and guidance in various types of service. Younger students are released from any service requirements outside of the school day. At their age, the focus is on learning how to conduct service, so teachers need to provide them with direct instruction with regard to this.

Teachers must guide students to explore the concepts of service and need. What is service? Why do we do it? To whom might we provide service? How does this benefit those individuals? To properly prepare students for service work, lessons can be taught about poverty and homelessness, living with disabilities, the challenges of aging, coping with natural disasters, and other issues concerning social justice.

At the high school level, service learning programs can focus on different aspects of service, including providing direct service, developing advocacy (learning how to speak on behalf of an issue that matters), and practicing philanthropy (investing monetary resources in social causes). In addition, older students can participate in a Youth for Justice Service Project—developing the ability to lead and problem solve with regard to issues of social justice.

Providing opportunities or requirements for students to work in the service of others brings benefits that extend far beyond the walls of the classroom. These activities bring students together and help them understand a greater purpose.

Providing Developmentally Appropriate Opportunities for Autonomy and Influence

Students should be given input into the disciplinary policies of a building and individual classrooms. Discipline procedures should be revisited before the start of each school year. It can be beneficial to periodically gather student input before determining what changes need to be made. Again, a survey can be used.

At Gamble Montessori, we were shocked when our student survey results indicated that students found "spreading rumors" to be a far more upsetting and damaging behavior than "physical aggression"—hitting, kicking, pinching, and so forth. As adults, we had all subscribed to the belief that physical attacks were certainly more damaging than psychological ones, but this was clearly not in accordance with the experience of our students.

As a result of this insight, a new disciplinary category was created entitled "psychological aggression," which included the spreading of rumors and making threats. This type of behavior was assigned consequences of equal magnitude to that of physical aggression. Without asking for information from our students, we would have never understood their perspective, and we would have made assumptions and decisions based on an adult understanding of peer interactions.

As is often the case, the best source of student information can be found simply by asking students.

Student government is another avenue where students can be given influence in myriad ways. This influence can include making decisions about such social events as pep rallies or prom, or larger concerns like dress code policies or discipline procedures. The specific change in policy is not the key component here; rather, it is the engagement of students in decision-making processes.

CONCLUSION

There are many ways to build community or school connectedness. When a program establishes common ideals; cultivates relationships; and provides opportunities for cooperation, service, autonomy, and influence it provides a sense of "what we do here." That, in turn, creates a place where students want to be. Having resilience, or a "positive, adaptive response in the face of significant adversity,"[9] is crucial for at-risk students, and a strong school community is a powerful component of developing resilience in students.

> Research on resilience gives educators a blueprint for creating schools where all students can thrive socially and academically. Research suggests that when schools are places where the basic human needs for support, respect, and belonging are met, motivation for learning is fostered. . . . When a school redefines its culture by building a vision and commitment on the part of the whole school community . . . it has the power to serve as a "protective shield" for all students and a beacon of light for youth from troubled homes and impoverished communities.[10]

What could be more powerful than creating schools where students belong, where they know "how we do it here," and where they want to be? What could be more powerful than providing a "protective shield" for students living in poverty or other stressful circumstances? Surely this has more lasting implications than testing ever could.

Callia is a hero. She was a focused and dedicated student who was also consistently kind to others and stood up against injustice. She was impressive in any circumstances but all the more so considering the additional factors she was dealing with.

One morning, Ms. Zane found her just after the bell rang, crying at her locker. This wasn't terribly unusual. Callia's parents were having marital problems. On several occasions, she had come to Ms. Zane in tears, wanting to discuss what had happened at home; this usually involved her parents yelling at one another, threatening to leave, and sometimes even collecting personal belongings, packing up a car, and saying good-bye to the children. Callia had been referred to school-based counseling services, and in the past when these events occurred, they would call home and get reassurance that the fight had blown over and all was well in the family. This allowed Callia some peace of mind and the ability to continue with her day.

Recently, however, things had escalated. Callia's father had arrived at the school office one morning with his arm bandaged. Callia's mother had stabbed him with a knife, and she was now in jail. Callia and her brother would be staying with her grandmother until things were sorted out. When Ms. Zane saw her at her locker, she thought things had gotten worse.

Ms. Zane approached Callia and asked what was going on, but she was crying so hard, Ms. Zane couldn't make out what she was trying to say. Ms. Zane brought her into her classroom for privacy and, upon further questioning, determined that this time, she was not upset about anything going on at home.

Callia told Ms. Zane that after arriving at the bus stop, she had to return home because she had forgotten her key. When she went back to the bus stop, the bus had already gone by. This was a very cold day in February. In fact, it was so cold—well below freezing—the school district had implemented a two-hour delay for buses of elementary-age students to protect them from standing at the bus stop in the dangerously cold temperatures. This policy, however, didn't apply to high school students, and Callia had missed the bus.

She could have returned home and not gone to school, but she didn't. Instead, she walked more than an hour to school. She was crying at her locker because she was tardy and afraid she had missed the departure for the field trip being taken that day. Ms. Zane immediately helped Callia take off her shoes and began warming her icy feet in her hands. Together they decided they would wrap Callia's feet in plastic bags and bundle them in extra socks. Ultimately, Callia got on the bus in time for the field trip.

Callia walked for more than an hour on a dangerously cold day just to be at school. For her, school was clearly a place where she belonged. She was a member of the Gamble community; she was able to face adversity, in part, because of the resilience she gained from a sense of school connectedness.

Students deserve a school where community is nurtured and valued, but for those students who are facing adversity, this fills a crucial need and provides essential protection.

TIPS OF THE TRADE

Cultivate Caring and Supportive Relationships

- Build schedules that allow teachers to stay with groups of students for more than a single year.
- Cluster students so they travel together between classes, developing smaller cohorts within the school as a whole.
- Require students to be present at parent–teacher conferences or other meetings where their school performance is being discussed with a parent or caregiver.
- Develop a positive relationship with parents/guardians.
  - Remember that regardless of the challenges that may be present, you are discussing their "most precious thing."
  - Find authentic things about which to praise their child.

Establish Common Ideals and Procedures

- Ensure consistency and clarity with common ideals and procedures to establish a culture and tone for a building.
- Define "what we do here" and give students values to identify with and work toward achieving.

Create Structured Ways for Students to Conduct Service Work

- Help students feel as if they are part of something bigger than themselves.
- Provide meaningful work and the opportunity to give back and be of use to others.
- Help adolescents discover their purpose and feel they are important. Engage students in direct service to help others in ways that are productive and proactive.
- Provide for direct instruction and structured and supervised opportunities to participate in service work. Without this guidance, the value of the work may be lost.

Provide Opportunities for Autonomy and Influence

- Allow students to have input into school decisions whenever possible.
  - For innocuous things, such as colors, names, and so forth, allow students to have complete decision-making control.
  - For more sensitive topics, collect student input and include it as part of the decision-making process
- Give students opportunities for leadership and responsibility on a regular basis.
  - Require self-care of spaces.
  - Allow student leadership of meetings or other classroom or community-based discussions.
  - Permit students to self-design celebrations, ceremonies, or other similar classroom events.

Creating a Climate of Interpersonal Respect

On a cold fall afternoon on the loading dock of an urban high school, bracketed by two scraped and dented yellow metal poles, stood two teachers. One was a beginning teacher, skinny and white, dressed just a bit more formally than everyone around him to avoid accusations of being a student. He was looking everywhere for a mentor. His current target, Roberta, was contemplatively smoking a cigarette, her fingers flicking ash absently toward the rookie, her other hand pinching shut the top of her jacket, which was cinched tightly around her waist. He had no idea she was headed out for a cigarette when he initiated the conversation, and he now stood shivering and jacketless next to her.

They were discussing a text by a black author and with a black protagonist. He was asking questions about aspects of black culture that had arisen, and she was providing monosyllabic answers. Certainly, his questions were ill-informed, however well-intentioned they may have been. Perhaps they were insulting. He does not remember many of her responses, save one, the one with which she dismissed him, forever: "You can never understand," she asserted. "You will never understand."

He felt stung. He believed in the power of the written word to convey the human experience, in the magic and lure of reading and writing. The Holy Grail he sought in every book he opened was to be able to honestly say about the author, "I know how she feels." He was insulted by Roberta's statement that he was incapable of understanding or that the well-chosen words of Toni Morrison, Zora Neal Hurston, and Alice Walker were incapable of conveying these truths. He invoked their names and held them up to Roberta.

"Are you really arguing that these authors are incapable of expressing their perspective? These women, among the greatest authors of our time, are unable to explain the black experience?" he argued incredulously. Roberta looked at her watch, dropped her cigarette butt on the dock, and ground out its flame with a twist of her foot. A diminishing cloud of cigarette smoke and the fleeting wave of her fingers underlined her dismissal as she briskly walked to the door.

THE PROBLEM

Since the settlers at the Massachusetts Bay Colony passed the "Old Deluder" law in 1647, compelling citizens to send their children to learn to read and understand the laws of the colony, schools have been our country's great meeting places. Public schools are inhabited by representatives of all economic classes of people, and since 1954, this has included all races as well. But our ancestry is not the only difference that can create interpersonal challenges. Our upbringing, socioeconomic status, and education also make up an important part of who we are and can color our interactions with others.

Personality differences can create conflicts as well. In his best-selling book *Emotional Intelligence*, Daniel Goleman suggests that we are hard-wired to not get along with about 20% of the people we meet.[1] This means that even within a homogeneous class of 30 students, the opportunity for social mistakes and misunderstandings among students and with the teacher are abundant.

Urban schools tend to have a great deal of cultural and racial diversity. It is typical for classrooms to have African American students, Appalachian students, Latinos, and students from a wide range of other nationalities and backgrounds.

How does one create a classroom and school community that is racially and culturally responsive—that is, where everyone feels valued and welcome—where there are so many cultures and personalities in the same small place? How does one find the time to address all of this? How does any person come to understand a culture that is different from their own?

Creating harmony from these different strains and songs of humanity—that is the goal of this chapter.

There are many "right answers" to creating a sense of community from a diverse group of people, and there certainly is at least one wrong answer. Imposing one culture on everyone, asserting that it is "understood" to be the "norm" and then giving a small group of people the power to enforce it, is a wrong answer. Americans have used the term *melting pot* since the publication of Alexis de Tocqueville's letter in the 1830s popularized the phrase. The suggestion is that people of all backgrounds, races, and ethnicities will, in the United States, simply blend together through marriage and education until ultimately all that will separate us is a middle name revealing a secret ancestry.

That is a dramatic oversimplification of the imagined effects of global migration. If you eliminate any vestige of culture, the thinking goes, there will be no opportunity for misunderstanding. A shorter version is, "Make everyone speak English." While this sounds achievable as a technical goal, it is not necessarily a desirable outcome. No social setting can be scrubbed clean of culture, and if it were to happen, there would be a loss of creativity, a loss of perspective, and a loss of the ability to truly innovate to overcome seemingly insurmountable obstacles.

If the melting-pot approach happens in the classroom, the teacher asserts a set of rules based on her experience and culture, and pronounces them to be examples of the universal experience. Instead, they are merely representative of her experience. She has set herself up as the judge of how to eliminate our differences and which behaviors are acceptable or unacceptable. Students from different cultures and backgrounds find their habits and choices derided, and families feel that school is saying their choices at home are unacceptable. Discounting a student's culture, and thus a parent's role, is a road map to educational disaster.

In reality, it is our differences that make us more than merely the object of curiosity but which extend us to a greater sense of what it means to be human and challenge our concept of equality. Culture infuses every action, rule, and conversation in the classroom. The teacher's and students' cultures, a blend of manners, beliefs, and responses to stimuli, will seep through whatever rules and codes are imposed. Thus, instead of pretending the differences do not exist, they should be called forth and celebrated.

Nonetheless, we must still find a way to work together in close proximity on important tasks, sometimes in high-stakes situations.

THE RESEARCH

The Los Angeles Unified School District Los Angeles Regional Adult Education Consortium's website reports that that there were 93 languages, one of which was English, used in the Los Angeles Unified School District in 2013. While this is obviously an extreme example of the extent of diversity available in some schools, it points to the challenges in creating a sense of cohesion among students and staff in an individual school, or even in an individual classroom.

African American students, especially black males, face a bevy of challenges in schools. Foremost among these challenges, they are disproportionately assigned the strongest consequences for misbehavior. Nationally, they are assigned the highest consequences at a rate almost 2.5 times that of their white peers who commit the same offenses.[2]

Although this data has been used to suggest that African Americans are more prone to misbehavior, what it really shows is that when they misbehave the same way as their white peers, they are far more likely to receive the highest consequence. It is the consequence—assigned by the adults in charge—that shows evidence of bias. These higher consequences, one of which is expulsions, track closely with incarceration statistics. In the United States, one in every three black males is likely to end up in jail in their lifetime. Many of these jail terms come for committing the same crimes for which whites receive fines or other, lighter consequences.[3]

Conversely, students from Asian backgrounds face a fascinating variation on the Pygmalion effect, where the teacher's perception shapes the outcome as much as the student's behavior does. In many cases, these "model minority" perceptions about Asians mean they are placed in accelerated classes and expected to perform well academically. This can lead to greater achievement. This can also mean that Asian students are less likely to ask for help and be noticed when they are struggling. Students often live up, or down, to the expectations their teachers place on them.

These systemic differences in experiences shape one's educational pathway and affect one's outlook and likelihood of success. Minority students in the United States are more likely to grow up in poverty. Ultimately, the strongest correlate to a student's ACT score is not their race, or their school, or the number of AP classes they took—it is their parents' income level.[4] It is far more likely that behaviorally (as well as academically), these students find themselves the beneficiaries of high socioeconomic status or victims of poverty.

Students who grow up in poverty face even more obstacles than their financially blessed peers. They have become habituated to lower expectations for their current actions and future outcomes, and separated from the pedagogy and language of expected success. Years of hardships and expected poor outcomes means that these students have a self-defeating script they are following, especially as they enter high school, and they must unlearn bad habits as they are learning new good ones.

Whether in Ashland, Ohio, or Los Angeles, California, schools are where these students of various backgrounds meet. The crucial edges of these boundaries, where poverty meets privilege and one culture meets several others, can create either exciting innovations or treacherous conflict. Misunderstandings are common, even expected, in these educational borderlands. It is not just students who are impacted by these difficult conversations and situations; teachers are also experiencing and processing these conflicts. Teachers desire to guide their students, but they often forget or fail to use their resources to prepare themselves. And the problems are daunting. Cultural differences run deep, infusing our actions and even determining the answer to moral conundrums.

Consider this dilemma: Suppose you are on a boat with your mother, your spouse, and your child. Suddenly the boat begins to sink. You determine that you can only save one of the other passengers. Who do you save?

Many who encounter this question consider the answer to be revealing of one's moral code; however, the answer reveals far more about one's culture than one's morality. About 60% of U.S. citizens determine they should save their spouse, with the other 40% saving their child. Many Americans assert that this is a moral answer, perhaps adding, as one respondent did, "Well, your parents are older and they should die first anyway." This feels like a comfortable rationalization for the tendency to save one's spouse and child.

This response stands in stark contrast to respondents in Asian cultures, who choose almost 100% of the time to do the thing most Americans would not: save their parent. With confidence equal to that of their American counterparts, Asian responders asserted that parents have the greatest value, as you are only granted one mother or one father, whereas a spouse or a child can be replaced.

This is a significant difference, with almost polar-opposite responses. It suggests that something believed to be as deep as absolute morality is instead dependent on the cultural norms in the culture from which one hails. Counting on one individual to be the holder of a moral absolute—whether it is regarding behavior, work quality, or skills mastery—is folly at best. It might, in fact, be something far worse. It may create an unintentionally prejudiced classroom where some students feel isolated and adrift, unable to put forth their best effort.

Even within "American culture" there are narrower subcultures, for instance, Appalachian, Asian, African American, Hispanic, and a host of other immigrant communities. For her book *Other People's Words*, Victoria Purcell-Gates conducted her research through the lens that "all learners are seen as members of a defined culture, and their identity with this culture determines what they will encode about the world and the ways in which they will interpret information."[5]

Accepting the premise that culture really shapes how we view everything, while working to achieve the goals of a school, means there can be no assumptions made about the culture of the teaching staff and student body.

What should be done in this case?

The school must work to create its own culture. This new, adopted culture must be shaped with an eye toward not offending or limiting the beliefs and values of the members' cultures. It also means confronting such big issues as racism and poverty head-on. That can be done by establishing special sets of rules for how we interact in almost every situation. This may sound impossible, but it's not. It is likely that several components are already in place at your school or in your classroom. It does, however, require an investment of time and energy.

Maria Montessori said, "It is not enough for the teacher to love the child. She must first love and understand the universe. She must prepare herself and truly work at it." This is deep wisdom.

The teacher must prepare herself, and she must prepare her students, for working together.

THE SOLUTION

The solution is to work together to develop a series of rules or codes for how you will interact with one another. Working together to formalize these processes, intentionally addressing the differences of culture, background experience, and socioeconomic status that can be brought forth, creates a multimodal definition of the culture "here." This process of developing the guides together creates a sense of shared purpose and values, and inevitably draws out conversations about not only the cultural differences, but also the deep philosophical similarities that can serve as a foundation for the group.

Examples of those sorts of codes are common in schools, businesses, sports teams, and essentially every organization that persists. Perhaps they are better identified not as "codes," but norms, core values, mission, and vision statements. Additionally, we propose creating and living according to a staff agreement.

Core Values

Almost every school and business has a set of core values. Often passed down from "on high," these were developed by past administrations and may seem immutable, like the Ten Commandments. These are often rewritten in times of turmoil or turnaround.

Kroger's website reports, "In fulfilling our commitment, we always live by our core values: Honesty . . . Integrity . . . Respect . . . Diversity . . . Safety . . . Inclusion," with each value followed by a concise definition of what that word means in an organization. The Build-A-Bear corporation reflects its core business repeatedly in its core values: "Reach, Learn, Di-bear-sity, Colla-bear-ate, Give, Cele-bear-ate." The childcare corporation Bright Horizons Family Solutions uses an acrostic, HEART: "Honesty, Excellence, Accountability, Respect, Teamwork."

Many schools have adopted similar sets of core values, and forward-thinking districts encourage this. Cincinnati Public Schools (CPS) is one large district that has encouraged each school to develop their own core values. This happened as part of the Positive Behavior Interventions work to reduce student misbehavior and the concomitant recidivism that comes when the sole answer to misbehavior is punishment. Creating core values as a positive vision to live up to—rather than depending on consequences to change behavior—helps provide a structure and purpose for right behavior to replace wrong behavior.

Within CPS, there are many examples of these core values. Gamble Montessori's values—community, hard work, learning, peace, and respect—were "stolen" from their sister school Clark Montessori as they attempted to model their program on Clark's historical success. CPS's Dater High School asserts, "At Dater High School, we . . . Work Hard, Love to Learn, Never Quit, Care, Prepare for the Future." Pleasant Ridge Montessori, another of the public Montessori elementary schools in Cincinnati, proudly proclaims "PRM ROCKS," which seems to suggest five core values; however, their core values are respect, ownership, kindness, and safety. (Yes, they are aware that this is really "ROKS.")

This points to the obvious truth about core values: The most important thing is to have them. The only wrong core values are the ones you don't have. There is not a right or wrong number—they can be as short as one (Google's "Don't be evil") or as long as 10, although that gets a bit unwieldy.

At Gamble Montessori, like many schools, the school asks (requires?) students to write a reflection when they have misbehaved. This reflection is a way to reteach appropriate behavior and help a student understand why they misbehaved. The reflection form requires the student to identify one or more of the core values that were violated by the misbehavior. Redirecting students to the core values not only serves as a reminder of the rules, but also helps them understand that the rules serve a purpose other than providing an annoying roadblock to doing whatever one pleases.

Instead, appropriate behavior is understood to demonstrate these easily remembered values, and misbehavior is defined as what does not match them. Hence, it is the core values themselves that guide how students are expected to behave, rather than a list of specific rules. This is a much better strategy for teaching behavior than trying to imagine the countless permutations of behaviors throughout the school and teach each individual scenario, as a student in a future new situation is likely to remember one of the core values and apply it to improve their behavior.

In 2016, at a Professional Learning Communities conference in Minneapolis, Minnesota, Learning Tree Solutions educational legend Richard DuFour stood in front of the group to perform what seemed to be a bit of a large-scale parlor trick. He told a crowd of more than 1,500 people that he knew the mission statement at each participant's school. He then proceeded to prove it.

"At Tree City school," he intoned, and the words appeared on the screen in front of us, "we will educate our students to meet their highest potential." He continued, to a wave of familiar laughter, "To meet or exceed academic goals." There was more laughter. "On the standardized tests," he added. The audience thought perhaps this was an aside, but the words showed up on the screen with the rest. "To be good citizens." It was starting to hit home. He *did* seem to know everyone's mission statement, and he ended with a familiar line: "And to become . . . say it with me . . . life . . . long . . . learners.'" They *were* able to say it with him. He had indeed captured the essence of pretty much every school's mission statement.

Maybe the mystery is why don't schools all have the same mission statement to start with?

Vision and Mission

A vision statement frames what your school will look like when everything is perfect—when all the pieces fall into place and you have achieved your goals. When developing a mission statement, groups ask themselves the following questions: What are we living into? What are we growing toward? What will the world look like when we have achieved what we set out to do? It is meant to be an aspirational statement about where your students, and possibly the faculty and parents as well, hope to be as a result of working together.

This does not have to be done at the school level. Individual classrooms or even groups of students can develop a vision for their own classroom. Doing so creates a sense of shared purpose that is as powerful at NASA as it is in an individual classroom.

At Gamble Montessori, the school vision statement is "Incorporating Montessori principles, we will create an enriching academic environment and a diverse, nurturing community that allows us to achieve our limitless potential." They have many of the components that Mr. DuFour addressed, although "lifelong learners" is replaced with "our limitless potential." The vision appropriately starts at the school's Montessori roots and passes through academics and their intent to create a nurturing community.

Ultimately, however, it is not much of a to-do list for achieving their limitless potential. It is a vision statement—where the school would like to end up. It is okay, however. The heavy lifting will be done by the mission statement.

It is okay for a vision statement to be imperfect or fail to check off all the boxes of a typical vision, or even if, in many ways, it is indistinguishable from someone else's. The important thing is that you have defined, as a classroom or school, where you plan to go.

A mission statement is closely linked with a vision statement, but it should describe the actions being taken to achieve the vision. Where the vision is a future objective, the mission is the steps you will take to get there.

It is okay that a given mission does not exactly fit the aforementioned definitions. If it did, we would all be Tree City. A mission statement does not provide a comprehensive list of correct actions to take or proscribe a turn-by-turn road map to helping students achieve their limitless potential. It should provide guidelines and moral underpinning for the work. What matters most is the process by which it was derived.

To create your mission and mission statements, there are important steps to be taken. The process described here is a good template; however, it does not have to be strictly followed in the form given. Your group of students or adults may need less—or more—structure to create a working set of statements. A seasoned teacher or facilitator should work from this template knowing she has the freedom to add or pull away restrictions based on the needs of the group.

First, find a way to involve everyone in the process, especially at the beginning and end. This can be done by having a meeting during contract time when everyone is required to be present or soliciting volunteers to come outside of contract time, with some sort of inducement to provide compensation for or reward their involvement. Alternatively, a less powerful process could involve circulating a straightforward questionnaire with two or three questions. This offers everyone in the organization a stake in the process. Include those in leadership positions, for example, a leadership team or board of regents.

Once you are together, ask yourselves, Why do we do what we do? What could it look like if we did it perfectly? These guiding questions, or survey questions, should form the heart of your final statement. You are in the aspirational phase, at the beginning. In effect, you are building a cathedral. Dare to dream. Only a stretch goal will force you to stretch.

Then, find words and phrases that begin to summarize or encapsulate the answers provided to the guiding questions. Pay careful attention to synonyms and nuanced words that incorporate positive and negative connotations. Do certain words keep coming up? Keep them. Are there specific words that summarize major concepts you heard in the gathering phase? Add them.

Next, wordsmith it in a small group, focusing on making sure it captures the spirit of your school. How can the ideas be stated more succinctly? How can the phrasing be shorter and more comprehensive? This work needs to be done by a small group rather than the entire group, because wordsmithing by committee is a Sisyphean task. The opportunity for miscommunication and frustration is too high in a large group, and many people will feel they did not have an opportunity for input.

This group should return with at least two but no more than five different "best shot" drafts. These should again be presented to the entire group, and a system of voting should be used. This voting system should be predetermined. Many times, in a discussion about the heart of an organization, people will propose a voting system that—in their calculation—will get them a desired outcome. Announcing the voting system in advance defuses this politicking.

The penultimate step is to formally adopt the statement that was voted on by the entire group. All schools have some sort of governing body, whether it is an instructional leadership team or a similar structure. Their imprimatur is an important step in this process. This is why you involved them from the start: If they are happy with it and the staff is happy with it, the rest of the process has a chance to work. If they are not involved in the process and at least satisfied that it was fair and inclusive, you have dragged your staff through frustration and conflict to simply spin their wheels. Finally, have someone formally present an executive summary of the process and product to the group responsible for approving it, and vote to formally adopt it.

Then all you have to do is live into it. Voilà! End of chapter.

Perhaps this last step requires further explanation. Living your vision statement seems to contrast with the daily work of teaching. In those moments of grading, correcting student misbehavior, differentiating lessons, or turning in grade summaries to the principal, "our limitless potential" seems a long way away. At the end of a long day, it is easy to lose sight of the cathedral you're building.

So, what is the solution? One key part is to never let the statements get too far from your consciousness. Post the vision and mission statements in multiple places, in plain sight from where you sit while grading. Place the core values on your handouts. Call forth the better angels of your nature at every opportunity as you are responding to students. Summon your courage and lean on these statements as you interact with colleagues.

These last interactions, addressing coworkers with issues related to core values, require one more key value statement, the staff agreement.

Staff Agreement

Core values and mission and vision statements are key components to establishing the culture in the school; however, they provide precious little guidance for how the staff will interact with one another. A staff handbook may provide technical clarity on what must happen or what is forbidden, but it does not address the bulk of interactions that happen between teachers and other staff on an ordinary day.

One school with a clear vision and mission, and five clear core values posted in every classroom, nonetheless found itself in the midst of a schoolwide storm. These statements, by themselves, are not a talisman to ward off conflict. Disputes and disagreements, sometimes strong and even seemingly foundational, are part of forming any team. These storms happen in cycles as teams form, change, and mature. Thus, living the core values is recognized by teacher leaders to be an adaptive problem, rather than a technical one. That is, even though the school had solved the technical problem of posting the core values prominently in the classroom and everywhere else, the hard work of aligning behavior, actions, and even word choice to those same values remained. More clearly, the teachers and administration at the school lacked the skills for resolving even small problems among themselves. These small problems then festered, with each one serving as a proxy battle for the last.

One leader stepped up to lead the staff in the process of developing a staff agreement. Functioning as a sort of user's manual for the mission statement, it would outline how to have those daily conversations that form the work of a school—and how not to have them. Leading this conversation takes significant thought and preparation.

After significant reflection, the leader, in one case, developed a plan that ensured the group would be able to do the following:

Focus on solutions, not problems. Getting bogged down with identifying problems only serves to distance teachers from one another and keep them focused on the negative.

Engage all participants to enhance buy-in. If the goal is to implement change, people must believe in what they are being asked to do; this is easiest when they have had the opportunity to give input.

Find a path to consensus. In some situations, making decisions by majority vote is appropriate, but something like this requires that everyone is on board.

Provide enough time to allow for a thorough process. It is not helpful, and can be detrimental, to open up a sensitive topic without the resources of time and energy to see the conversation through to resolution.

Generate something substantive. It is not enough just to come up with good ideas; there must be some kind of visual repository or tangible product developed from those ideas.

The following is the step-by-step process the leader used to help extricate the staff from the whole-building storm they were experiencing.

Step 1: *Name the elephant.* Like most schools, hers had all kinds of rules and processes for helping students understand how to interact with one another but nothing that guided the adults. This meant that when they were experiencing stress, they had no protocols to turn to for assistance. The staff needed to create expectations for themselves. The first step was simply to identify this as a need and something that would benefit everyone.

Step 2: *Brainstorm.* Each participant was asked to record on index cards three explicit actions or behaviors they believed they needed or wanted from their colleagues. The provided prompt was, "What do you most want/need from your colleagues?" The specific directions were to record as many as three specific actions or behaviors, phrased positively, each individual wanted from their colleagues. Each suggestion was to be written on a separate index card to allow for sorting in the next step.

Step 3: *Identify commonalities.* The index cards were collected, shuffled, and redistributed to small groups. Each group went through their stack of cards, identifying responses that were similar and determining the weight of each category based on the number of comments on that topic. This served several purposes. It gave participants the opportunity to anonymously see one another's responses, allowed common threads to begin to emerge, and, most importantly, got everyone engaged in working collectively on the task.

Step 4: *Consolidate and find common language.* Each group reported their conclusions, and the things that had been identified as important to the majority of people became apparent based on the number of responses, which were tallied. The leader worked to ensure that individual voices were heard and honored, while maintaining the value of seeking consensus from the group.

Step 5: *Create a tangible product.* After the group discussed, clarified, and compromised, they created a final summary statement to identify what was most important in establishing and sustaining beneficial interactions with one another.

See Figure 4.1 for a sample staff agreement.

The faculty was creating a staff agreement, and the decision was made to allow word choice to be debated. Although this can derail the process of determining mission and vision, it was deemed to be important to work though word choice disputes for the staff agreement. The group, predictably, argued about the importance of specific components.

Just as predictably, they touched on old, long-buried arguments and, at times, stepped on one another's feelings. This part of the process was much like tiptoeing through a minefield. Some people were in that same minefield, stomping their feet.

There was a moment that had the potential to derail the process. An angry debate arose about the importance of including a statement about cultural differences. Several staff members felt it was crucial to explicitly state the importance of honoring cultural differences, while others believed it was implied in the components. It was, they believed, an unnecessary addition that duplicated earlier statements.

This argument was indicative of the struggles they had been experiencing as a group. It reflected power struggles and initially arose like an intentional challenge to the process itself. It was too simple, some believed, to simply blame our conflicts on cultural differences. Of course, a statement on cultural awareness was an appropriate thing to include in the agreement. With hindsight, the leader expressed her disbelief that they had argued about a decision with such a clear correct answer. The statement stayed.

The facilitator wisely allowed the discomfort to be felt and used it as a catalyst, while not becoming sidetracked or allowing the work to devolve into a battle between competing agendas. She had the hardest job, listening hard, carefully restating positions, and negotiating personalities and old conflicts, while always pushing toward the goal of establishing shared expectations.

Ultimately, the staff agreement served to remind teachers of ways to take care of their relationships with one another.

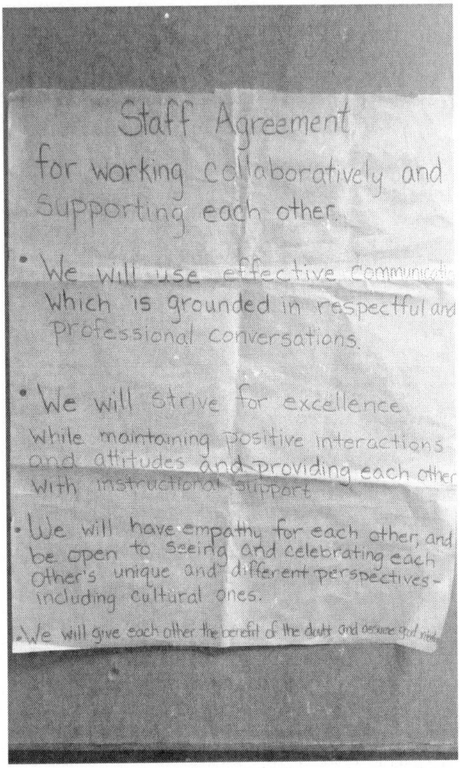

FIGURE 4.1
Sample Staff Agreement

In the brilliant movie *A Few Good Men*, a trial revolves around whether the commanding officer ordered a "code red," an unofficial punishment, which led to the death of a marine. During the trial, the defense provides a witness with a binder of rules and procedures for the base. The witness is challenged to find a "code red" in the binder of regulations for Guantanamo Bay. He is unable to do so, and the defense turns him over to the prosecution. In a pivotal moment, the prosecution redirects to the same binder, asking the same witness to find the mess hall. He responds, essentially, that everyone knows where it is.

This proves an important point about the culture and functioning of any place, whether a military base or school: Often the most important aspects do not make it into the staff manual. This absence of clarification is especially prone to happen to something as hard to define as culture and the nature of interpersonal interactions. But this is the cement that holds an organization together and merits as much attention as, say, the dress code.

CONCLUSION

Culture pervades everything we do. Schools and classrooms cannot escape this and should not try to erase an individual's culture. Instead, seek ways to celebrate these personal differences, while constructing guiding statements and policies to create a school culture that allows for productive interaction.

A group of seniors had organized a walk through their neighborhood to raise awareness about abusive relationships and encourage other teens to escape from such relationships. The group of 20 or so walkers that had gathered was comprised almost entirely of African American students and family members. They were milling around in the lobby, talking to one another and waiting for the signal to start. The principal, a white man, recognized a former student in the group and spoke to him familiarly.

The principal's stomach growled. He had postponed lunch because he knew that following the walk there would be a lunch of green beans, mashed potatoes, wings, and his personal favorite—homemade fried chicken. He was about to make a big mistake as a white guy standing in a crowd of black individuals. He asked his former student, a young black man, "Tell the truth: You're here for the fried chicken, aren't you?" As if hitting a switch, the group got noticeably quieter. The principal immediately realized what he had done. He had just blurted out a statement that matched a common offensive stereotype about black Americans.

Years of working among various cultures drew him back to the core values developed at the school—values familiar to the students and parents around him. He thought about peace and respect, and about taking responsibility for his own choices. Without skipping a beat, he owned his comment and addressed the likelihood that it had been offensive, saying, "Oh my God. That sounded really racist, didn't it?"

The student laughed, nodded, and said, "Yes, it really did."

The principal added, "I just said that because I, myself, am here mostly for the fried chicken. I heard Malaya's mom can really cook."

From behind the principal came a voice that said, "She can cook, but it was *my* recipe. And you can have two pieces." There was laughter, a reprieve—a reprieve made possible by the principal's efforts to understand and participate in a culture different than his own, and a reciprocation from an understanding walker.

TIPS OF THE TRADE

Really *Use* the Core Values, Mission Statement, Vision Statement, and Staff Agreement

- Before each staff meeting, use one of the values statements—core values, mission statement, vision statement, staff agreement—as a reflection piece. Some schools add other core pieces, for example, a district statement about inclusionary practices or nondiscrimination policies.
- Post the statements in the classroom. Placing attractive and legible versions of the values statements in a prominent place in the classroom helps provide a framework for the expectations in your classroom. This is strengthened if the values are posted throughout the school and as they are used in the following additional steps.
- Use the statements in your classroom and school rules. Relating each of your classroom rules to the core values, perhaps using each value as a "header" with specific rules beneath it, moves you toward several important goals. First, you justify each procedure or rule as belonging to a larger structure of rules, giving each a raison d'être. Second, it helps students categorize each expectation, which aids their memory and makes it more likely the rules will be remembered and followed.
- Place the statements throughout the staff manual and student handbook. Core values can help serve as an organizational structure for your handbooks. Much like with the classroom rules, using them as an organizer helps justify rules and expectations. Placing them here also ensures they will be

seen at least once a year as you review the expectations with your staff and they, in turn, review the expectations with their students.

- Include the statements in student reflection forms.
- Refer to the statements constantly in disciplinary conversations. Your student reflection sheet should ask students, "Which core values were broken?" The student is then prompted to explain how specific values were broken. (Interestingly, the frustrated student sometimes goes to great lengths to explain how another student, or even the teacher, violated a core value. That works too.)
- Use the statements on student commitment forms. Many schools ask students and parents to make a series of commitments as they enter the school or progress to new teams. This is certain to include following the rules and not committing certain infractions. It may also address doing work of a certain quality and exhibiting exemplary behavior. Using the core values in this document, especially in combination with those items mentioned earlier, helps send a unified message to students.
- Use the core values on your school letterhead and other public sites. The core values should saturate your school. The message you send outside the school is important, too. Showing partners, parents, and others that you have a thorough commitment to your values sends a message that a school has thought about what it expects from students. Beginning with the end in mind is an attractive trait to parents who might have to wade through a wide range of choices or be seeking reassurance that their only choice is a good one.
- Place the statements in new and unusual places—on teacher appreciation mugs, T-shirts, screen savers, the price board at the football field concession stand, and so on. You get the idea.

Create a Responsive and Welcoming Culture in your Classroom

- Standardize and teach the rules of grace and courtesy in your classroom. This softens the edges and creates space for being gentle when we make mistakes. Some examples of classroom expectations that are not cultural impositions are as follows: Expect polite language, even in common interactions; practice what to do in common classroom situations, for instance, when someone drops something fragile or loud, two students bump into one another, two students disagree on an important issue, or a class is divided over a thorny topic. Provide a place or time for students to talk to you individually to address concerns about something that has happened.

- Teach students how to mediate their own differences and include the practice of stating the other person's position.
- Get to know one another. Getting to know your students and coworkers, and letting them get to know you, is key. Attend sporting events and school concerts; personally call and invite parents to open houses and student-led conferences; provide chances for personalization in assignments by allowing students to choose what they research for assignments; and ask questions about student interests, perhaps using a start-of-the-year survey. Then build responses into lesson plans however you can or go to such nonschool events as church functions where students will be performing or visit them at work.
- Learn about other cultures, both individually and as a class, by reading books by or about people from other countries and groups, especially those represented in your classroom, intentionally diversifying readings and experiences, perhaps by asking, What cultures and countries are you interested in learning about? and working cultural and ethnic studies into your thematic lessons.

5

Discovering How Misbehavior Reveals Unmet Needs

The first day of school is always fraught with anxiety for teachers and students alike, and this feeling was intensified for Ms. Ostin, as she was just beginning a new position. Other teachers had already warned her about Malia, who was returning to a general education classroom from a program for students with behavioral disorders. Many had hoped that Malia would remain in the behavioral placement for the rest of her high school career.

Although this pessimism unnerved Ms. Ostin, it didn't sway her from committing to trying to build a positive relationship with Malia. To ensure that they got off to a good start, Ms. Ostin approached Malia's desk and extended her hand to introduce herself. Before the words were even out of her mouth, Malia turned away, facing the wall, and said, "I don't like teachers."

This was not an auspicious beginning. *"I don't like teachers."*

Those words hurt. Ms. Ostin felt a natural reaction to respond to being hurt by hurting back. But instead of acting on that feeling, Ms. Ostin continued to cheerfully greet Malia by name each morning, day after day.

Throughout time, it became clear that Malia had the potential to be a good student and wanted Ms. Ostin to see this in her. Woven between bouts of being disrespectful, Malia shared insightful comments, and on the days she did her work, she demonstrated good understanding.

It was certainly not smooth sailing, however. Malia was involved in verbal and physical altercations far too often, and her grades fluctuated based on her emotional stability. But by the end of the first semester, she was spending significant time in Ms. Ostin's classroom after school. Despite Malia's challenges, she managed to pass the year and move on to 11th grade, and even the naysayers had been convinced to let her continue in the general education environment.

Ms. Ostin moved on to another position, and although Malia was no longer in her class, they remained in contact. Several years after Malia graduated from high school, she sent a message to Ms. Ostin:

> You have touched so many students, including me. If it wasn't for you, and helping me when I needed, then where would I be. When I was on an IEP I never thought much about it or never got the help that I needed until you came along. I thank you for that. I was so heartbroken when you left, but I knew I had to keep positive and work toward graduating. Even after you left, you still supported me. Coming to my choir concerts, etc. Thank you for always being there when I wanted to give up or when I wanted to be stubborn just because. Lol! You taught me a lot. XOXO

This from the girl who had once so rudely turned away saying, "*I don't like teachers*"; however, the greatest and most beautiful irony occurred several years later, when Malia decided to pursue a degree in education. Perhaps someday, she will, in turn, profoundly impact a struggling student.

THE PROBLEM

Teaching is at least as much art as it is science, and paying attention to student needs requires vigilant application of artistic skill. Most public school classrooms are comprised of 25 to 35 students, each of whom arrives at school each day with an abundance of needs—such tangible needs as school supplies, a lunch, or a Band-Aid, as well as intangible ones, like a check-in, a hug, a word of caution, or, like Malia, just plain old-fashioned attention.

How can teachers possibly recognize and address all of these needs and teach content, too? While this may seem impossible, making a conscious effort to pay attention to student needs every day might be enough.

Every teacher has a story about a student who has challenged their authority and openly pushed them away. We often react by feeling hurt or experiencing anger or self-doubt. Traditional educational pedagogy seems to validate this personalized reaction—the assignment of rigid consequences, removal from class or school, and zero-tolerance policies are all in alignment with this idea that disrespect of authority and failure to follow expected procedures must not be tolerated.

Students must be held to high behavioral expectations; that is not negotiable. But it is equally important that teachers understand that these displays of disrespect, these apparent "rejections," are often opportunities to see a student's vulnerability and misguided invitations to establish connections. This is part of the art of teaching—the ability to step back from the moment of interaction and examine the subtlety contained in the big picture.

What is the student telling you that is not being directly spoken? What clues are available in tone and body language? What can be inferred through an examination of situations that have occurred previously? What outside information about the student could provide insight into the current behavior? It is only through this careful and conscientious examination of the broader context of the interaction that the deeper message can be discerned.

THE RESEARCH

This concept, that misbehavior provides clues related to unmet needs, is not a new one. It dates back to the research on mistaken goals conducted by Alfred Adler at the turn of the 20th century. Adler's ideas were later expounded

Table 5.1. Mistaken Goals Chart

The child's goal is:	*If the teacher feels:*	*And tends to react by:*	*And if the child's response is:*	*The belief behind the child's behavior is:*	*Coded messages:*	*Proactive and empowering responses:*
undue attention (to keep others busy or get special service)	annoyed; irritated; worried; guilty	reminding; coaxing; doing things for the child he or she could do for himself or herself	stopping temporarily but later resuming the same or another disturbing behavior	I count (belong) only when I'm being noticed or getting special service; I'm only important when I'm keeping you busy with me	notice me; involve me usefully	Redirect by involving child in a useful task to gain useful attention; ignoring (touch without words); saying what you will do and "I love you and ____" (e.g., "I care about you and will spend time with you later"); avoiding special service; having faith in the child to deal with their feelings (don't fix or rescue); planning special time; establishing routines; engaging the child in problem-solving; establishing nonverbal signals
misguided power (to be the boss)	challenged; threatened; defeated	fighting; giving in; thinking, "You can't get away with it" or "I'll make you;" wanting to be right	intensifying behavior; acting defiant; showing compliance; feeling he or she has won when the parent or teacher is upset, even if he or she has to comply; displaying passive power	I belong only when I'm the boss, in control, or proving no one can boss me around; you can't make me	let me help; give me choices	Redirect to positive power by asking for help; offering limited choices; avoiding the urge to fight or give in; withdrawing from conflict; being firm and kind; acting rather than talking; deciding what you will do; letting routines be the boss; removing yourself from the situation and calming down; developing mutual respect; setting reasonable limits; practicing follow-through.

revenge (to get even)	hurt; disappointed; disbelieving; disgusted	hurting back; shaming; thinking, "How could you do such a thing?"	retaliating; intensifying; escalating the same behavior or choosing another weapon	I don't think I belong so I'll hurt others in the same way I feel hurt; I can't be liked or loved	I'm hurting; validate my feelings	Acknowledge hurt feelings; avoid feeling hurt; avoid punishment and retaliation; build trust; use reflective listening; share your feelings; make amends; show you care; act, don't talk; encourage strengths; put kids in same boat.
assumed inadequacy (to give up and be left alone)	hopeless; helpless; inadequate	giving up; doing for; overhelping	retreating further; acting passive; failing to show improvement; providing no response	I can't belong because I'm not perfect, so I'll convince others not to expect anything of me; I am helpless and unable; it's no use trying because I won't do it right	don't give up on me; show me a small step	Break down the task into small steps; stop criticism; encourage positive attempts; have faith in the child's abilities; focus on assets; don't pity; don't give up; set up opportunities for success; teach skills and show how but don't do for; enjoy the child; build on his or her interests.

Source: Jane Nelson and Lynn Lott, "Mistaken Goals Chart," Positivediscipline.com. Retrieved March 27, 2016, from www.positivediscipline.com/sites/default/files/mistakengoalchart.pdf.

upon by his colleague, Rudolf Dreikurs. Adler and Dreikurs identified four "mistaken goals" that lead to misbehavior: undue attention, power, revenge, and assumed inadequacy.

The premise of their philosophy is that when children misbehave, it is a misguided attempt to fulfill the essential need of humans for belonging. "Children are social beings. Thus, their strongest motivator is the desire to belong socially."[1] When children are struggling to demonstrate appropriate behavior, they indicate an underlying feeling of a lack of belonging and the mistaken use of inappropriate behavior in an attempt to belong.

The theories of Adler and Dreikurs have continued to be studied and used by psychologists, parents, and educators. A helpful resource when applying this philosophy to educational practice is the "Mistaken Goal Chart" (see Table 5.1). This table identifies the behaviors typically associated with each of the four mistaken goals, a description of the mistaken goal, adult feelings and behaviors that often occur in response to the related misbehavior, and strategies to assist the child in regaining an appropriate sense of belonging through meeting the underlying needs the behavior is concealing.

It should be noted that students generally demonstrate a range of behavior that falls into multiple "mistaken goal" categories; however, there is often a predominant category in which a student's behaviors tend to cluster. Through the observation and awareness of the emergence of this pattern, teachers can begin to address underlying needs. The surface-level benefit of this is that the misbehavior will be reduced. However, the lasting benefit is that the child's needs are being met.

SOLUTIONS

When the Mistaken Goal Is Revenge

Years after her experience with Malia, Ms. Ostin had a similar exchange with another student, Jasmine. Again, Ms. Ostin was new to the building. She was an intervention specialist coteaching in a classroom that had a substitute teacher in for the general educator that day. Jasmine had her hand raised, so Ms. Ostin called on her. Jasmine responded by saying, "No. I don't need you. I need the real teacher." The *real* teacher? The *substitute real* teacher?

As with Malia, Jasmine was showing blatant disrespect, but, as also was the case with Malia, after diligent efforts at building a relationship, Jasmine, too, became a student who spent extra time with Ms. Ostin and maintained contact with her long after their time together was finished, returning regularly, often on weekends or holidays, to help out in the classroom and touch base.

Establishing these relationships required Ms. Ostin to see beyond the initial hostilities and look deeper to see the underlying needs being revealed through the behavior. Ms. Ostin could have taken a more traditional approach, relying on punishments and consequences to address the misbehavior. But had she done so, she would have merely reinforced these students' belief that schools and teachers were untrustworthy and punitive. This conventional response would have likely only escalated the problematic behavior, leading to an increased level of disrespect and a subsequent lack of academic engagement and success. Thus, the downward spiral would continue.

While initially it appeared that both Malia and Jasmine were pushing teachers away, in actuality, both of them were crying out to be noticed and desperate to be accepted for who they were—problems and all. Both students exhibited behavior indicating their mistaken goal was "revenge"—the behavior was an attempt to hurt others or get even; Ms. Ostin's related feeling was hurt. The underlying belief associated with this mistaken goal is, "I don't think I belong, so I'll hurt others as I feel hurt. I am incapable of being liked or loved."

With Malia and Jasmine, Ms. Ostin followed the advice of Adlerian disciples: Show you care, encourage strengths, and avoid punishments and retaliation. With this in mind, it seems unsurprising that, over time, both young women ultimately spent a lot of time with her and became strongly attached. Their outward behavior may have been demanding that she keep her distance, but what they were actually saying was, "Help me belong. Love me unconditionally."

This is not the same thing as, "Allow me to behave in any way that I wish" or "Like everything I do." There is a common misconception among children and adolescents that being cared about and supported is the same as being given permission to do as one pleases. This is by no means the case. Rather, guiding students toward true belonging and loving them unconditionally requires holding them accountable for their behavior, while providing correction in a way that keeps the behavior separate from the person. Although "what you do" may not be acceptable, "who you are" always is.

Knowing students as individuals is a key part of deciphering their needs, but this can be nearly impossible when teachers, especially those at the high school level, are working with as many as 180 students in the course of each day. This is precisely why misbehavior is an effective, if problematic, way for students to demonstrate needs.

Student misbehavior is difficult to ignore, and it increases in intensity if the underlying issues are not addressed. Students rarely present these needs overtly; it takes a lot of courage and insight, more than most students possess, to identify problems and ask for help. More often than not, teachers need to infer these needs based on exhibited behavior concerns.

This ability isn't something that is taught in teacher training programs. Perhaps it can't be taught. Perhaps this is what makes teaching more art than science. Additionally, it can't be measured. None of the bubble tests students take; the data talks they engage in; or the multitude of scores that will be aggregated and disaggregated to determine a student's progress, a teacher's worth, and the effectiveness of a school will ever come close to measuring a teacher's ability to pay attention to student needs. Yet, it remains crucial to an educator's success, because if underlying needs are not addressed, none of the instructional components the high-stakes bubble tests try so hard to quantify will matter.

If a teacher doesn't pick up on, and address, the peer conflict that happened on the way into the building, at best, those two students will spend the day far more focused on their social concerns than what they are being taught, and, at worst, the situation could escalate into a physical altercation. If a teacher doesn't quickly notice a student whose behavior is becoming increasingly problematic and try to redirect that energy into a more positive focus, the remainder of the bell could be spent battling for that student's cooperation.

And the girl who won't make eye contact as she enters the room and has a history of cutting her arms? It's critically important that someone notices her. Any educational theorist will tell you that pedagogy, methodology, and data analysis are the kingpins of education, but to that girl, on that day, the only thing that matters is that someone sees her need.

To effectively determine needs, teachers must receive and analyze a constant stream of sensory input. It is often cited that teachers make as many as 1,500 education-related decisions every day; teachers also take in and process a tremendous amount of information. I would argue it is one of the reasons teaching is so fatiguing.

Teachers need to be engaged with what is happening in every area of the classroom at every moment. That attunement comes through making connections with students. These interactions are rarely momentous. Rather, they take place in the human exchanges teachers have with students day after day. It is through these interactions that patterns of behavior are revealed and underlying needs can be discerned.

When the Mistaken Goal Is Power

It isn't always easy to make connections with students. Andre is an example of an extremely challenging student. He stole, lied, was noncompliant, yelled, cursed, and threw things. According to the Mistaken Goal Chart, Andre was expressing (loud and clear) the mistaken goal of power. He demonstrated intense behavior, a desire to be in control and emerge victorious from every conflict regardless of the cost. The belief behind this behavior is that the only way to belong is to be in control; students demonstrating this mistaken goal respond to challenges with a "You can't make me" attitude.

Students like Andre can be so disruptive many schools readily discard them through suspension or expulsion, or simply by "counseling them out." While these approaches may provide a solution for the school, they do not provide a solution for the student. The gains of using misbehavior to determine unmet needs become exponentially larger when trying to understand the unspoken needs of the most challenging students in a classroom or school. In these instances, the benefits of this practice may be nothing short of life-changing.

Moving from program to program typically only leads to even greater instability and increased problematic behavior. It is important that schools make every effort to keep students in their building, even when that's difficult. It is only through maintaining consistent relationships that teachers can effectively perceive students' needs, and understanding needs helps effectively address behavior.

There are no disposable students. Removing a child from a situation where the staff is familiar to one where she or he has no connection sends a strong message of being unwanted; however, for these challenging students, behavioral change is hard and takes a tremendous amount of time and patience.

Mr. Hayman made little progress the first year with Andre. Andre's behavior remained difficult, highly disruptive, and sometimes even dangerous, resulting in a significant amount of time where he wasn't in school due to disciplinary action. But during the second year, there were glimpses of change.

Every year at Andre's school, junior high students take a fall camping trip to get to know one another and develop cohesion within the community (see chapter 7). In seventh grade, Andre's problem behaviors were such that he was unable to participate in the trip; however, during his second year, Andre skated through and got to go on the trip.

As part of camping preparation, Mr. Hayman taught a lesson on local wildlife. This lesson must have stuck with Andre, because he became the wildlife scout at camp.

His excited cries of, "Mr. Hayman! Mr. Hayman! Is that a wild turkey?" or "That was a vulture, right? I can tell because it has raggedy wings," were heard regularly at camp.

Andre spotted hawks, turkeys, and vultures. He situated his canoe in the front of the flotilla and, as a result, was able to see seven great blue herons. And on the third day, he proclaimed, "Mr. Hayman, come here quick, I think that's an eagle." It was a bald eagle, to be precise.

Andre shined bright at camp. His teachers saw his strengths. He demonstrated leadership. He helped others. He was engaged in hands-on learning. This was the perfect opportunity to address Andre's need for power. At camp, there were limitless opportunities to allow him to be in charge in positive ways, to invite him to help rather than require he comply. What a gift it was to be in a setting where he was motivated to engage in cooperation rather than the constant redirection he required in the classroom, which regularly created a battle for control. Andre's teachers would have missed this entirely if he had been prohibited from participating in the trip again, and he certainly exhibited behaviors that warranted doing so.

This camping trip was a pivotal moment of connection. But it did not ensure smooth sailing. Student growth rarely occurs as a straight line. Rather, it is a topsy-turvy curlicue that regularly curves in on itself and only can be viewed as evidencing positive change over time. Andre continued to struggle with behavioral expectations, but gradually, the positive moments became more regular.

One day during the spring of his second year, Andre came to Mr. Hayman in tears. (This was nothing short of shocking, as Andre was hardly thin-skinned.) Another teacher had kicked him out of her classroom that day because of his behavior. Andre reported that she had added insult to injury by stating she hoped he would leave the school. This may or may not have been true, but the important piece was that it bothered Andre deeply.

A year earlier, Andre would have said he didn't care and likely cursed at this teacher, leading to an escalated situation and more severe consequences. This time, he did nothing of the sort. He wanted to stay at his school, and he wanted to be wanted. Instead of immediately reacting, he sought out Mr. Hayman. They talked and thought of some solutions to the problem, and Andre was able to return to class the next day. This was real change.

By his third year, Andre's successful days outnumbered his difficult ones. He was by no means a model student, but he was normalizing and beginning to look more like a typical adolescent than a child destined for jail. When he moved on to high school the following year, he remained connected with his junior high teachers. At the end of the first quarter of his freshman year, he asked the school secretary to put copies of his report card in their mailboxes. He had made the honor roll for the first time ever.

Andre's story is an example of a student expressing a powerful need for belonging and a teacher who paid attention and put in the time and energy necessary to begin to fulfill that need. Andre's journey with Mr. Hayman was long and difficult, but by seeing his problem behaviors as a cry for help—a mistaken goal evidencing a desperate need for belonging—Mr. Hayman was able to help Andre see a different vision for himself. Andre, however, did the hard work of beginning to grow into this vision.

When the Mistaken Goal Is Assumed Inadequacy

Students like Andre who are in crisis will often behave in a manner that is impossible to overlook; however, every student deserves a teacher's careful attention, even if they are seeking it in a less overt manner. It is a mistake to think perceiving the needs of "average" students is simple. By definition, "average" means the norm, and thus the most standard of experiences.

In fact, these "typical" students are most likely to fly under the radar and go unnoticed. As a result, they may be the most in need of a teachers' intentional and careful powers of observation. The insights gained from this lead to the development of an understanding of less-extreme underlying needs. In turn, having this understanding creates a more positive teacher–student rapport.

Aisha was a dynamic young woman who was high-spirited, energetic, and boy-crazy. In eighth grade, she was not an exceptional student, academically or socially. She was the kind of student who could easily get overlooked or even discounted. Mrs. Martinez was frustrated with her because by this point in her academic career, she should have been exhibiting stronger leadership skills in the classroom. Instead of guiding the younger students in this multiage classroom to demonstrate model behaviors, she was allowing herself to be drawn into their immaturity.

Mrs. Martinez spoke with Aisha about this on many occasions. Aisha was always chagrined, but nothing seemed to change her behavior or issue a strong enough invitation for her to rise as the leader she was capable of being.

Based on Adler's Mistaken Goals Chart, Mrs. Martinez's feelings of "helplessness" were a clue to Aisha's mistaken goal of "assumed inadequacy." This goal is aligned with a student's belief that she is helpless and incapable; there is no point in trying for improvement because there is no hope of getting it right.

But then, halfway through second quarter, Aisha made a fortuitous mistake. She skipped one of her classes two days in a row. Mrs. Martinez learned about this from a colleague with whom she regularly collaborated. While not pleased about the behavior, Mrs. Martinez knew it was an opportunity to push the envelope with Aisha—a chance to provide the wake-up call Aisha needed.

At the first opportunity, Mrs. Martinez put on her best "disappointed teacher" face and pulled Aisha out of class for an individual conversation. She told Aisha she was a role model and a leader in the classroom (although this was not entirely true, Mrs. Martinez used this moment to acknowledge Aisha's potential and her faith in Aisha's ability to achieve it) but that her current behavior was not aligned with the positive young woman she knew and expected Aisha to be.

Aisha was remorseful and apologized. But the most powerful moment came when she tearfully said, "I don't know why I skipped class. I don't do that. I don't lie to teachers." She recognized the person she had really betrayed was herself. She cried. Mrs. Martinez cried. They hugged and moved on.

It was important that Aisha and Mrs. Martinez experience the full cycle of the conversation, moving from anger and disappointment to acceptance and rejuvenation.

According to Adler's theory, when students demonstrate the mistaken goal of assumed inadequacy, adults can instill more appropriate behaviors by showing faith in them and sending the message that their teachers won't give up on them.

The incident between Mrs. Martinez and Aisha profoundly impacted the relationship between the two of them. Aisha had to experience Mrs. Martinez's deep disappointment in her before she could trust that Mrs. Martinez wasn't going to give up on her, even when she made a mistake. Mrs. Martinez could have simply assigned Aisha to Friday Night School—it certainly would have saved time and energy—but, had she done that, Aisha would have only gotten half the message: that Mrs. Martinez was upset with her and that her behavior was wrong. This was the least important half; the most important aspect of their interaction was the acknowledgment at the end that they were still in this together and that Mrs. Martinez still believed in her.

Consistent enforcement of clear discipline policy is important, but used in isolation, it does not reap this deep benefit. It is only through the time and energy put into authentic and engaged human interaction that real understanding is experienced, and this is where the most effective change and growth can occur.

Aisha did not suddenly become the dynamic classroom leader Mrs. Martinez knew she could be, but she got closer. Knowing Mrs. Martinez wouldn't give up on her if she made a mistake or was unsuccessful allowed Aisha to risk taking on leadership roles, even when she was worried she couldn't live up to them. In addition, Mrs. Martinez understood Aisha better. The relationship they had established made it much easier for Mrs. Martinez to understand and anticipate Aisha's underlying needs.

The time spent establishing a relationship was recouped in saving time dealing with misbehavior later on. This is the instructional benefit gained from delving into the needs that underlie every student's behavior, and at one time or another during the course of a school year, teachers will likely have the opportunity to see this side of each of their students—even those who are typically considered "highly successful."

When the Mistaken Goal Is Undue Attention

Neil was a highly successful student. His critical thinking skills and knowledge base were several grade levels above those of his classmates. He was highly intellectual, well read, and had a supportive home environment. Neil was going to earn good grades and high standardized test scores without much intervention from his teachers; however, the mission statement at Neil's school noted the importance of developing students into "thoughtful, intelligent, inclusive human spirits who contribute to the stewardship of the community and planet."

Neil had some growing to do in this area. He loved to participate in class; he often challenged his peers and teachers to think more deeply about a subject or question commonly accepted information or beliefs. But he also wanted to be called on all the time, sometimes for the sole purpose of proving someone else wrong. He struggled to understand why he couldn't provide all the answers and was regularly frustrated with his classmates' slower pace of learning and limited background knowledge. Additionally, Neil hated group projects. He insisted he could do better work on his own and was likely correct in this claim.

Neil seemed to always have his hand raised. When called on, he often used a corrective or argumentative tone with both teachers and peers. When others were called on instead of him, he openly indicated his displeasure. During group work, he regularly made negative comments about his peers or took over the work so he could complete it to his specifications. His seemingly constant need to have attention drawn to him was an irritant to his teachers and classmates alike. His behavior felt annoying and grated on everyone's nerves.

Collaboration and the ability to work with people who are different from you is a crucial life skill and is aligned with the school's mission. Neil's academic giftedness couldn't be allowed to stand in the way of his needed development. Differentiated instruction and curriculum compacting assisted with managing some of his frustration by challenging him academically; however, removing his struggles entirely would not have helped him build skills in the other necessary areas. In fact, supporting him through these challenges was more beneficial for his development as a "thoughtful, intelligent, inclusive human spirit" than simply placing him in an accelerated program with other students like himself.

Based on Adler's Mistaken Goals philosophy, Neil was exhibiting an underlying need to gain undue attention. Teachers most certainly felt "annoyed" and "irritated" by his behavior. Arguing with Neil was ineffective; he could engage in debate like an experienced defense attorney.

In the case of a student seeking undue attention, Adler notes the adult should not "fix or rescue." Neil had to figure out how to work in groups. He had to develop tolerance for not being called on in class. This meant it was in his best interest for his teachers to refrain from removing him from these experiences or save him from experiencing the discomfort involved in them. Despite his protestations, Neil continued to be assigned group work, and he continued to experience the frustration of not always being called on in class.

Adler also recommends involving students like Neil in useful tasks and planning special time for the child. Neil loved being perceived as the class expert. When a teacher asked him to verify information or help explain a complicated concept, Neil was able to use his tremendous mental bank of information to enrich the group. In this way, he learned strategies for sharing his gifts without demeaning or criticizing others.

Moreover, Neil needed to be given opportunities to engage in conversations and interactions at an adult level. Often, his topics of interest and dry sense of humor were not understood by his peers; he needed an outlet where these gifts could be acknowledged and appreciated. Planned "special time" either through brief hallway exchanges or lengthier lunchtime conversations helped Neil feel connected and understood. This helped establish a positive rapport so that Neil was better able to receive corrective feedback about his behavior in the classroom.

When students' underlying needs are examined, it makes it easier for teachers to nurture the whole child and focus on developing skills that are far broader than those that merely engender academic success.

CONCLUSION

Managing student misbehavior may be the most difficult part of teaching. Establishing rigid consequences and/or removing students from the classroom or school are tempting palliative quick fixes. They at least temporarily stop the disruption—a short-term fix. This is clearly a common trend. "During the 2011–12 school year, the U.S. Department of Education counted 130,000 expulsions and roughly 7 million suspensions among 49 million K–12 students—one for every seven kids."[2]

Nevertheless, removing students from the classroom and school negatively impacts students' sense of belonging, causes them to fall behind academically and socially, damages teacher–student relationships, and does little to effect positive behavioral change. These short-term punitive approaches often not only fail to help children improve their behavior, but also can serve to exacerbate it.

That is the exact opposite of what is needed for a long-term solution—both from the perspective of managing a functional classroom and helping students become happy, healthy, well-adjusted adults who are productive members of society. There are few, if any, teachers who would state this isn't the ultimate goal of teaching.

When viewed through the lens presented by Adler, student misbehavior is a misguided means to address an unmet need. If teachers only focus on the behavior without examining the unspoken needs that are driving the behavior, the problems will continue to occur and likely escalate, especially when handled only according to traditional discipline codes.

Directly addressing the unmet needs and teaching students alternate methods to meet these needs assists with the challenging work of classroom management and actively works to change behavior. This strategy teaches students that the adults around them are working to help them be successful, rather than simply punishing them for their failures.

The self-confidence of children and adolescents can be tenuous, fragile, and fleeting. They need as many people looking out for them as they can get. Pay attention to needs. See misbehavior as a form of communication. Look for mistaken goals and proactive ways to address them. Provide students with the critical sense of acceptance and belonging they so longingly seek.

It is easy for student needs to get lost in the shuffle of standards and objectives, as well as data and paperwork. Noticing these needs, seeing misbehavior for what it really is, and effectively responding to it is truly an art. And it is this, not test scores, grades, or maybe even curriculum, that students will remember.

TIPS OF THE TRADE

- Q-TIP = Quit Taking It Personally. Much of the time, student behaviors are related to other things going on in their lives. Teachers play the role of a safe adult who regularly provides clear and consistent correction. Sometimes students will use the classroom as an environment in which to act out because it is a secure place where they can get their needs met. Teachers better serve their students when they can detach themselves from misbehavior. This is much easier said than done, but correction is far more effective when teachers and other school staff members are able to avoid personalizing problem behaviors.
- Use behaviors, in conjunction with the Mistaken Goals Chart, as a tool to gather insight into student needs. When students are acting out, ask yourself the following questions:
  - Is there a pattern to the behavior?
  - What leads to the behavior?
  - What purpose does the behavior serve?
  - What is the student getting?
  - How can you help the student achieve this purpose without evidencing the behavior?
- Although misbehavior can be frustrating and challenging, fight against the natural inclination to push difficult students away. Provide opportunities that allow students to shine—remembering that sometimes this happens most clearly outside of the classroom.
- Seek out every opportunity to build relationships with students. This happens gradually and takes time, but every interaction counts. While the development of relationships with students is not considered a "measurable outcome" on a bubble test, it is a required precursor to academic gains. The

following are some everyday strategies that help with relationship development:

- Smile and greet students every day.
- Ask about students' interests, hobbies, or even just how their weekend was.
- Check in with students when they seem down.

- Find the good, and praise it. Actively and intentionally seek moments for students to see themselves as their "best self."
  - Provide positive feedback at every opportunity.
  - If you struggle to find anything positive, look harder. See past the challenges. Remember, you are issuing an invitation—a possibility for them to grow into.
  - Be careful to avoid backhanded praise. Steer away from such qualifiers as, "When you don't ________________, it is really wonderful to work with you," "Even though you usually ________________, this time you ________________," or "I really liked when you ________________, but often you ________________."
- Remember behavioral change takes time. You are planting seeds. Whether you get to directly witness the fruition of your labor, know that you are laying the groundwork that may someday allow students to make better choices.

6

Designing Instruction to Create an Inclusive Environment for All Learners

Tilesha stopped by Mrs. Evans's room to chat one day after school. After a few moments, she nervously shared that her mom was talking about having her transfer to a high-performing school in the district that required an entrance exam for admission. Tilesha is a student who would be successful in such a program; however, Mrs. Evans realized she wasn't just sharing information. Tilesha was looking for feedback and worried about potential disapproval for considering changing schools.

Mrs. Evans first talked to Tilesha about the things the selective school does really well and the potential benefits she could gain by transferring there. And then she shared with her what Gamble does really well.

When Mrs. Evans began talking about leadership skills—and Tilesha's emerging leadership, in particular—Tilesha's eyes lit up, and she said, "You mean like how we help each other and how we make sure everyone feels included?"

Mrs. Evans acknowledged this was exactly what she meant. She especially noted how at Gamble, students recognize the value in every individual, regardless of academic ability.

Tilisha looked puzzled. She said, "Wait, do they even have students like Gary (who has Down syndrome) there?"

Mrs. Evans reminded Tilesha that since high test scores are required for admission, they do not accept students like Gary.

Tilesha's response speaks volumes about the power of inclusion and belonging: "Well, why not? I mean, that's terrible. How do students learn how to help one another and work with people who are different from them if they can't even go to school there? That makes me sad."

Tilesha (see the following insert) immediately recognized the loss to high-performing students like herself if she were to attend a school that accepted only the most academically successful students. Although much of the literature on the highly debated topic of academic tracking focuses on the potential costs to struggling learners and the potential benefits to gifted students, Tilesha saw this as a cost to the growth and development of every student, including herself.

While discussion about how to group students for instruction may seem like a by-product of the current, standardized testing, one-size-fits-all approach, student grouping models have been a widely discussed topic dating back to the turn of the 20th century. Over the years, there have been many theories about, and strategies developed for, grouping students to best meet academic needs, but ultimately the debate may boil down to a single essential question: Is it better for students to be grouped homogenously with others of similar skills and abilities or heterogeneously with others of disparate skills and abilities?

Tilesha had a clear opinion based on her personal experience. A long-standing analysis of the data definitively supports her statement. Yet, this debate has raged on for more than 100 years.

THE PROBLEM

Classrooms are comprised of individual students. Each of these children arrives with unique academic and developmental needs. Teachers are not only charged with getting every student to master the grade-level standards and objectives, but also expected to meet the individual learning needs of each student, providing enrichment or remediation where appropriate. To grasp the full magnitude of this task, it is important to understand the demographic makeup of the public school classroom in the United States as it relates to academic ability.

The 2014–2015 report of the National Center for Education Statistics notes that in public schools in the United States, there are 6.6 million students receiving special education services; this amounts to 13% of the total population of public school students. Almost 65% of those students spend more than 80% of the school day learning in the general education setting. In fact, only 10% of special education students spend more than 60% of each school day outside the general education setting.

On the other end of the academic spectrum, students identified as gifted and talented make up 6 to 10% of the public school population, and most of them also spend their instructional time in the general education setting.

Of course, in between these two extremes lie the remaining 79% of "typical" students. These students, too, have a wide disparity of academic needs and abilities. In light of this, achieving standards mastery and meeting students' unique needs seems like a daunting task indeed. It is a task that, on its surface, may appear impossible and certainly makes homogenous (ability) grouping seem like a tempting option, if for no reason other than making instruction seem more feasible. And yet, the data clearly cautions against this.

THE RESEARCH

Grouping students by ability has seen many incarnations throughout the years: academic tracking, between-class grouping, XYZ grouping, the Joplin plan, self-contained special education, honors programs, advanced placement, gifted classes or schools, and within-class groupings. For accuracy, it is helpful to define each of these models.

- *Academic tracking:* Ability- or achievement-based determination for assignment to a course of study (primarily seen at the secondary level).

- *Between-class grouping:* Ability- or achievement-based determination for classroom assignment (primarily seen at the elementary level).
- *XYZ grouping:* Based on a model begun in 1919, in Detroit, Michigan, IQ scores were used to place students into one of three tracks, identified as X, Y, and Z. This model would be deemed unconstitutional if attempted today.[1]
- *Joplin Plan:* Ability- or achievement-based determination for placement in cross–grade level ability-based groups for math and/or reading instruction only (used at the elementary level).
- *Self-contained special education classes:* A separate classroom explicitly for students with disabilities.
- *Honors:* Classes or courses of study explicitly for high-achieving students.
- *Advanced Placement:* Often an offshoot of honors classes; students have the opportunity to earn college credit for these courses based on an end-of-course standardized assessment.
- *Gifted classes or schools:* Programs or classes exclusively for students identified as gifted or talented.
- *Within-class groupings:* Small, homogenous instructional groupings that exist within a heterogeneous classroom environment.

Regardless of the name given to it, each model places students into a group based on either a single measure, for example, an IQ score, or multiple measures, for instance, past performance. The rationale behind this is the idea that if students are grouped by ability or achievement, the teacher is better able to target instruction to meet the needs of the group.

But the implementation of instructional strategies should be based on student growth and development, rather than ease of instruction, and the data simply does not support homogenous groupings.

Major meta-analyses of the research on this topic, conducted first by Robert Slavin, and again by Kulik and Kulik, found that, overall, there are no benefits of tracking-type models. "The achievement effects of ability-grouped class assignments are essentially zero."[2] What this means is that while there were some academic benefits seen for some students, there was an equal negative cost to other students. This is a significant finding; the gains for some students come at an equal expense of others. If there is no net gain for ability-grouped models, why does this remain such a pervasive practice?

It should be noted that both meta-analyses found small benefits to within-class groupings and cross-grade groupings (Joplin Plan) for reading and math instruction only. These findings were seen only at the elementary level, as, historically, both of these grouping models are seen only in elementary classrooms. Both sets of data also note more significant gains for gifted students when provided with a separate, accelerated curriculum.[3]

It is these gains for academically talented students that prompt parents, particularly those who are well-educated and more affluent, to push for these types of separate programs for their children; however, whatever academic benefit this type of grouping brings has significant costs for students slated for the average and lower-level tracks. Students assigned to these types of groupings are not only less academically successful, but also they demonstrate greater negative perceptions of school, exhibit more discipline problems, and have reduced goals in their expectations for higher-level education.[4]

Achievement gaps between students assigned to different tracks were, in fact, greater than those between students who remained in school and those who dropped out after the 10th grade, indicating that tracking of students creates greater achievement outcome disproportions than those between students in school and those who do not complete high school.[5]

This disparity has concerning societal implications as well. As Jeannie Oakes states in her book *Keeping Track: How Schools Structure Inequality*, "Tracking separates students along socioeconomic lines, separating rich from poor, whites from nonwhites. The end result is that poor and minority children are found far more often than others in the bottom tracks."[6]

Jonathan Kozol takes this a step further, noting,

> It's not just that tracking damages the children who are doing poorly, but it also damages the children who are doing very well, because, by separating the most successful students—who are often also affluent, white children—we deny them the opportunity to learn the virtues of decency and unselfishness. We deny them the opportunity to learn the virtues of helping other kids. All the wonderful possibilities of peer teaching are swept away when we track our schools.[7]

This is exactly what Tilesha so clearly understood simply by virtue of her own experience. The data indicates that homogenous groupings are an ineffective, and likely damaging, educational practice. Yet, they remain a pervasive model, especially at the secondary level. Tracking of some or all classes is evidenced in almost 75% of all middle schools.[8] High school programs tend to have even higher levels of this.[9]

It is easy to understand why this is the case. Teaching students in heterogenous groupings is challenging, so challenging that despite decades of evidence in favor of it, homogenous models continue to be more the norm than the exception.

THE SOLUTION

Education is a service-based profession centered on people, and people will never fit into a one-size-fits-all model; however, when we intentionally separate people, we create stratification and reinforce difference. The middle ground here lies in the implementation of differentiated instruction. Because while the research on grouping structures stands firmly against tracking (or tracking-like) models, it indicates benefits for homogenous groupings that are flexible, fluid, occur only some of the time, and provide adjusted curriculum for the students within them. This is true at both the elementary and secondary levels. When implemented fully, this is what differentiated instruction is—the means through which students with a broad range of learning needs can benefit from a diverse classroom environment.

At Gamble Montessori, during Shauna's first week as a seventh grader, her teachers already had concerns. When she was given a world map and asked to place the oceans and continents on it, she created it upside-down and identified the oceans as continents and the continents as oceans. In math class, she was so overwhelmed she tended to shut down and sometimes was brought to tears.

Shauna was one of those students who was compliant and likeable, and somehow skated through elementary school without the severity of her learning deficits being recognized. By seventh grade, they had become notable. It did not take long before her teachers began putting supports in place.

Shauna responded rapidly to interventions and differentiation. She became a powerful self-advocate, regularly double-checking with teachers that she had been provided with modified work. Through her openness and engagement with what she needed, she also became a terrific peer role model for normalizing the experience of having learning needs.

Early in her eighth-grade year, her teachers were able to reduce some of the supports she had been receiving. When she was given her packet for the first major writing assignment of the year, she promptly approached the intervention specialist and proclaimed, "Ms. Schulman, I got the wrong packet."

"No, you didn't," Ms. Schulman replied.

"Yes, I did," she responded. "I'm supposed to have the one with the sentence starters."

"Not anymore. You've made a lot of progress. We're moving you up," said Ms. Schulman.

Shauna's eyes grew wide, and she shook her head, saying, "No. No, I can't. I'm not ready."

Ms. Schulman smiled and said, "Yes, you are. I know it, and if you need help, I'll be right here."

Shauna continued making progress, and by the end of her eighth grade, she was ready to move up another level with her writing. More importantly, she felt confident in what she was able to do. During the course of two years, she had progressed from an introverted student who felt incompetent at tackling grade-level work to a student who believed in her abilities, trusted her teachers to guide her, and was rapidly moving toward grade-level expectations.

Differentiated Instruction

Shauna's story emphasizes the power of differentiated instruction. Nonetheless, there is no denying it is hard work. While it is true that planning differentiated lessons and assignments can be like preparing multiple lessons for each class, it is important to remember that differentiation is more of a process than a product. As Carol Ann Tomlinson states, "The pursuit of expertise in teaching is a career-long endeavor. They [teachers] aren't sprinters expecting quick success, so much as marathoners in the race for the long haul."[10] Too often, educational pedagogies are thrown at teachers with the expectation of immediate, full implementation.

Like all instructional practices, it takes time to develop expertise with differentiation. Teachers must be given, and must allow themselves, years to grow into this practice. The work of differentiation is one for the "long haul."

Getting started, or doing more, with differentiation can feel like a daunting task. It is important to keep in mind that differentiation is not a goal in and of itself. Rather, meeting students' needs is the goal, and differentiation is the vehicle. So, begin with planning.

There are many ways to differentiate—differentiated expectations, differentiated instruction, differentiated assignments, and differentiated assessments (see Figure 6.1). Add to this the ideas of differentiating based on complexity of task (vertical differentiation) and differentiation based on method of demonstrating proficiency, often called choice work or menus (horizontal differentiation), and suddenly, every lesson can begin to look like a Myers–Briggs personality-type chart. But don't despair—most lessons don't require differentiation of every type, and some lessons don't need to be differentiated at all. This is why it's so important to start with planning. See the example provided in Table 6.1 of a differentiated unit plan.

Begin by thinking about the standards and objectives for a lesson. Consider what students will need to meet the objectives. It is not necessary to differentiate every lesson. If it is an introductory lesson, an easily accessible concept, or a cooperative-learning-based assignment, it may be best for all students to engage in the work in the same way. But if this is not the case, consider whether it is the expectations, the instruction, and/or the formative and summative assessments that will require differentiation.

For example, if the lesson is introducing a new vocabulary unit, it may be that all students are best served by singular, whole-group instruction, but the assessment may need to be differentiated; however, if the given lesson is factoring polynomial expressions, the teacher may need to present this concept using different pacing and different materials for different students such that the expectations, the instruction, some of the assignments, and the assessment may need to be differentiated.

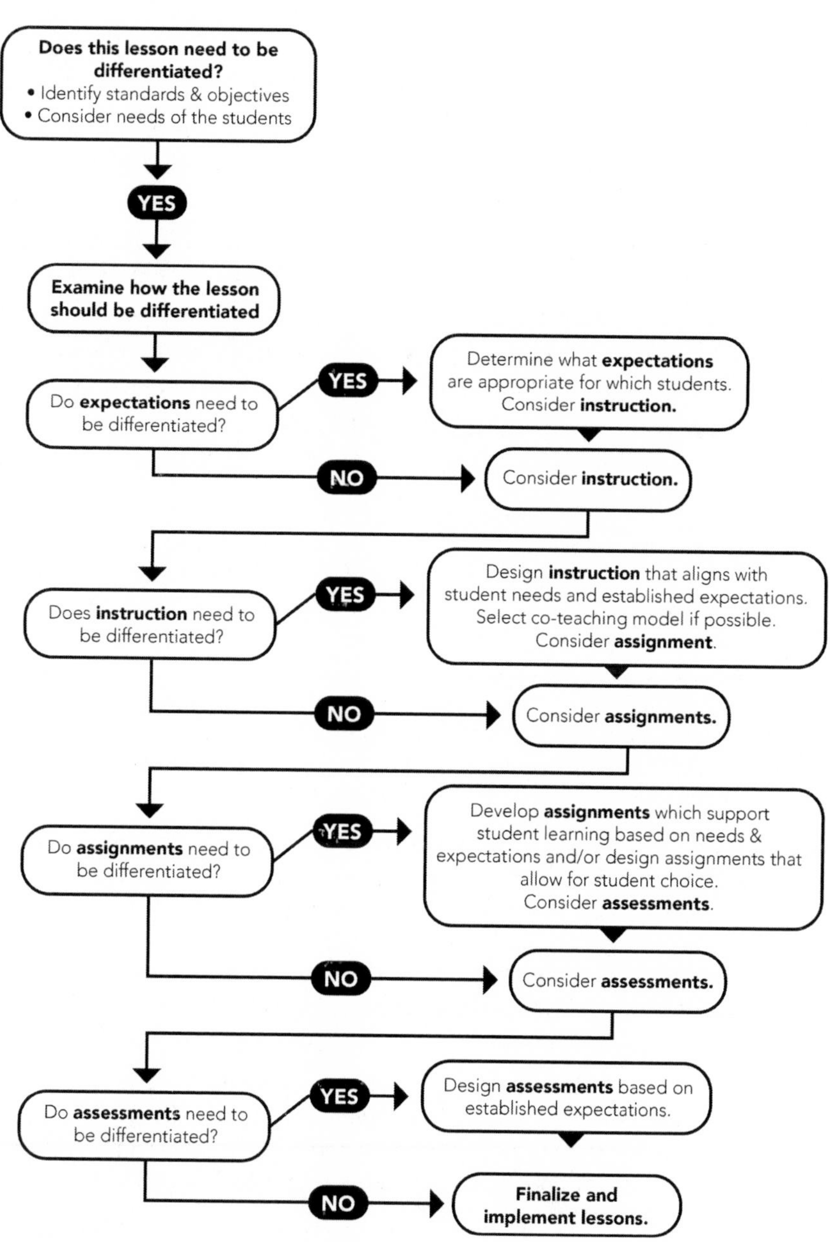

FIGURE 6.1
Flowchart to Help Determine Which Lesson Components Require Differentiation

Each time a teacher prepares to differentiate a lesson, the work begins with the needs of the students. This is what distinguishes differentiation from the traditional notion of such fixed, within-class groupings as the familiar "Bluebirds, Robins, and Cardinals" strategy. A student who has difficulty with reading comprehension but is terrific at memorizing is likely to excel at the vocabulary lesson. A student who is strong in mathematical reasoning but has poor retention of multiplication facts is likely to need additional support for the factoring polynomial lesson.

The fluidity in grouping that results from this careful consideration is one of the things that helps students not feel stigmatized by differentiation. Another component to this is the frequency of differentiation. When instruction and assignments are differentiated on a regular basis, this becomes part of the classroom culture.

At Gamble Montessori, in Mr. Williams and Ms. Tippett's class, differentiated work is provided multiple times a week. It is standard practice for this classroom, and students are very familiar and typically quite comfortable with this. Students will regularly ask, "Is this assignment differentiated?" or "Did I get the right level?" Additionally, they know that when work is handed out, there may be different directions on a paper or different structural supports provided in a packet. This is discussed openly, and most of the time students are very accepting of it.

But one spring, several students noted feelings of discomfort with the level of work they were receiving or comments their peers were making related to leveled assignments. This was unusual. Mr. Williams and Ms. Tippett could have chosen to directly address this with students, reminding them that ridicule and put-downs were not acceptable; however, they were concerned this would merely serve to drive the comments underground, rather than actually resolve the issue.

Instead, they chose to adjust their practice. For the next major differentiated assignment, they gave students the opportunity to self-select their level. Students were provided with a document describing the tasks and various available supports. The students recorded what level they believed they needed and handed this in.

Together, Mr. Williams and Ms. Tippett reviewed the student responses. With few exceptions, students had self-selected the same level their teachers would have provided them. Where teachers and students differed, Mr. Williams or Ms. Tippett wrote comments on the survey documents.

One example was, "You are welcome to choose this level. You will need to make sure you are organizing your essay in a way that makes sense, as the outline here is not as guided as what you are used to. Please check in with one of us after completing the first body paragraph so we can talk about how things are going." Another example was, "You have strong writing skills. We want you to continue working at the higher level. We know you can do it. Please see one of us if you get stuck or need assistance."

The art in differentiating instruction is the careful consideration of the requirements of the lesson and the needs of the students. This is the beauty in the design, and it allows the teacher, or teachers, tremendous creativity. Nonetheless, it is also complex and requires practice and support. It is not something that can be implemented all at once but, like every change in practice, instead begins by taking the first step. Perhaps that means beginning by planning a single lesson that includes differentiated assignments or designing a long-range project that includes many of the components of differentiation.

Coteaching

Differentiation is challenging but rewarding work. There is no question that it is in the best interest of students. But teachers need support to embrace and fully implement this practice. One way to make differentiation easier is to adopt a coteaching model. Coteachers are able to share the extra work that comes with differentiation, and differentiation practices maximize the benefits of coteaching.

Most schools include a variety of teaming structures, and there are few educators who don't serve on at least one type of team in their building; however, coteaching is a special form of teaming relationship.

Coteaching is a lot like a marriage—albeit an arranged one typically lacking in the romance department. But like a family unit, two adults are responsible for a group of children, and like parents, coteachers spend a lot of time working together—often both in time spent providing instruction during the school day and spent planning outside of school hours. Coteachers share classroom living space and are dependent on one another to share the responsibilities of the team. Like a marriage, coteachers must learn to work together and tolerate one another's idiosyncrasies.

What Is Coteaching?

Coteaching is defined as two (or more) teachers who coplan, coinstruct, and coassess academic content provided to a single group of students at the same time. There are a variety of ways teachers can partner to form a coteaching relationship, but the most common coteaching pairing is comprised of a general education teacher and an intervention specialist (special education or gifted education teacher).

Coteaching is a means of meeting the needs of all students by providing both supports for struggling learners and opportunities for acceleration within the general education setting. This is aligned with the inclusionary practice goals of increasing access to rigorous curriculum, providing all students with learning that is tailored to their needs, and with the legal obligation of delivering instruction in the least restrictive environment. It also matches the research-based recommendation, described earlier in this chapter, of keeping students in heterogeneous groupings while adjusting curriculum to support their learning.

Why Coteach?

There are many benefits to coteaching for both the adults and children involved. The pairing of a general education teacher and a special educator brings together two crucial skill sets for effective classroom functioning.

While not set in stone, typically the general educator is the content knowledge expert, has experience with whole-group classroom management, possesses knowledge of student backgrounds, and is familiar with expected pacing guidelines. The special educator tends to have expertise in knowledge of the learning process, individualization of instruction, and understanding of legal issues and required paperwork, and maintains a focus on learning for growth. Specific benefits for students include the following:

establishment of a respect for differences

creation of a sense of belonging

improved self-esteem

increased attention

provision of peer models

development of broader friendships

Specific benefits for teachers are as follows:

enhanced instructional knowledge base

collaborative problem solving

shared responsibility

increased grouping options

engaged teamwork

heightened creativity

ability to provide individualized instruction

See Table 6.1 for an example of how coteaching can be used to support differentiation practices in the classroom.

Models of Coteaching

There are six basic models of coteaching. Each model has specific benefits and rationales for implementation. Much like differentiation practices, the determination of which model to use depends on the standard being taught, your goals for your lesson, and the needs of your students.

The Primary Three Models

Team Teaching

This is often the model people picture when coteaching is discussed. In team teaching, two teachers share the same instruction for a single group of students. This model is best used when there is a clear benefit to having two people provide content. Examples include finding two ways to solve a math problem, enhancing instruction with two different perspectives, and using lessons that involve compare and contrast. While it is tempting to become overreliant on this method because it is often enjoyable to teach with another adult, this should only be used when having two teachers providing instruction enhances student learning.

Table 6.1. Sample Unit Plan for Including Multiple Forms of Differentiation

Unit: Comprehension of Informational Text

Standard/Objective/Concept: By the end of the year, students will read and comprehend literary nonfiction at the high end of the grades 6–8 text complexity band independently and proficiently.

Rationale for Differentiation: This task requires the ability to tackle text using strategies for literal, inferential, and analytical comprehension. All students need exposure to or practice with all strategies.

Coteaching Model: Station Teaching

Time Allotted: 225 minutes. 45 minutes each for:

- explanation of task, packet distribution, read and annotate text
- first station
- second station
- third station
- assessment

Level	*Expectations*	*Instruction*	*Assignments*	*Assessments*
struggling learners	With little support, students will be able to answer questions related to comprehension of literal text, citing evidence to support their response. With teacher and peer support, students will be able to answer inferential questions, citing evidence to support their response.	Read-aloud support for text annotation task (with intervention specialist). All stations teacher-led, with support for independent practice. (Intervention specialist leads literal and inferential comprehension stations. General educator leads analytical comprehension station.)	Assignment not differentiated. Student packet includes grade-level informational text passage, lesson materials, and practice questions.	Assessments not differentiated; however, grading of assessment is. Heavier grade weighting on literal and inferential sections of the assessment.

grade level learners	Students will be able to independently answer literal comprehension questions, citing evidence to support their response. With minor teacher and/or peer support, students will be able to answer inferential comprehension questions, citing evidence to support their response. With moderate teacher and/or peer support, students will be able to answer analytical comprehension questions, citing evidence to support their response.	Annotation of text and literal comprehension station are conducted independently. Inferential (with intervention specialist) and analytical (with general educator) stations are teacher-led; support available if needed for independent practice.	Assignment not differentiated, Student packet includes grade-level informational text passage, lesson materials, and practice questions.	Assessments not differentiated; however, grading of assessment is. Grade weighting equally distributed across sections of the assessment.
accelerated learners	Students will be able to independently answer literal comprehension questions, citing evidence to support their response. Students will be able to independently answer inferential comprehension questions, citing evidence to support their response. With little teacher and/or peer support, students will be able to answer analytical comprehension questions, citing evidence to support their response.	Annotation of text and literal and inferential comprehension stations are independent. Analysis station provides teacher-led instruction with general educator, followed by independent practice.	Assignment not differentiated, Student packet includes grade-level informational text passage, lesson materials, and practice questions.	Assessments not differentiated; however, grading of assessment is. Heavier grade weighting on inferential and analytical sections of the assessment.

Parallel Teaching

In parallel teaching, each teacher provides instruction to approximately half of the students. The resulting reduction in the student–teacher ratio provides the powerful benefit of small-group instruction for all students. The two groups can be carefully constructed to best facilitate differentiated instruction. There are times when parallel teaching is best done using heterogeneous groupings (e.g., small-group discussion) and times when it is best used for homogenous groupings (e.g., new content instruction provided at different levels of complexity).

Station Teaching

Having two teachers present in the classroom enhances the benefits of traditional station teaching. It allows for two teacher-led stations or for one teacher to lead a station, while the other teacher monitors on-task behavior and supports station transitions.

The Supporting Three Models

Alternate Teaching

In this model, one teacher provides instruction to the group, while the other teacher works with a smaller group to provide preteaching, reteaching, or remediation. The intention of this model is that the pullout group instruction is brief and carefully timed to allow for the least impact due to missed content. Once the support has been provided, the students return to the whole-group setting.

One Teach, One Collect Data

While this model may be most frequently used to prepare for special education paperwork, this does not have to be the case. There is tremendous value in data collection—including data collection of all students and data collection on effective teaching practices. When coteaching partnerships are grounded in trust and collaboration, they are the perfect relationships in which to observe one another, collect and analyze data, and make adjustments to instructional practices.

One Teach, One Assist

This model, where one teacher provides content instruction and the other provides support to students as necessary, is the model most frequently used and the one that is the least effective for student learning. While it is often the place where coteaching teams begin their practice, it should be moved away from as soon as possible.

It can be a helpful model to use while teachers learn how to blend their work, since it allows both teachers to learn the teaching styles, expectations, and routines and procedures of the other. It also provides time for the special educator to develop comfort with the instructed content and the general educator to learn effective strategies for working with students with disabilities.

At Gamble Montessori, the following words were spoken by a general education student to a special educator implementing a coteaching model: "Mrs. Brown, you must be the smartest teacher because you teach both math and language arts." This so clearly demonstrate that, to this group of students, the intervention specialist was as much a content teacher as the general educator. She was not someone who just helps out in the classroom, not the "IEP teacher" or the teacher of "those students," but, quite simply, one of the math teachers and one of the language arts teachers.

Along with this acceptance of the special education teacher as just another classroom teacher comes the mirror belief that the students who receive special education services are just regular members of the classroom community. There is no doubt that both of these pieces are the direct result of the implementation of coteaching models in the classrooms at Gamble.

Getting Started with Coteaching

While the benefits of coteaching are profound, there are many common pitfalls. Effective coteaching takes time and effort. Sharing your livelihood with someone else requires the development of trust. After all, coteachers are together in a classroom all the time. They are constant observers of one another's practice. They must support one another with classroom management and academic expectations. Most importantly, they share responsibility for a group of students. They must be able to rely and depend on one another.

In strong coteaching partnerships, instruction is so fluid teachers can often finish one another's sentences, and an observer in the classroom might not be able to recognize which teacher carries which job title, but this ideal does not happen overnight. Coteaching teams should expect three years of teaming before the model reaches full implementation; however, even a single year or semester of partnership can yield dividends for everyone involved.

CONCLUSION

In today's classrooms, differentiation, and the use of coteaching to support it, is not so much an instructional option as it is an ethical responsibility. The vast majority of classrooms represent diverse communities of learners—the presence of this diversity is a key component to the growth and development of all students as they become conscientious citizens of the world, but it also creates some inherent instructional challenges.

When tracking is rejected as an acceptable model—after all, "separate but equal" was thrown out as an appropriate option in 1954, with *Brown v. Board of Education*—what remains is the conundrum of how to educate students with a disparate range of skills, abilities, and experiences in the same classroom. This is a reality in the vast majority of classrooms throughout the country, and it is not something that is going to go away. Nevertheless, this should be seen as a great blessing and an opportunity, rather than an insurmountable difficulty.

Many teachers initially embrace differentiation practices as a means to support students who are struggling, as this is often a teacher's greatest challenge. But many people—especially affluent white parents—remain concerned about the impact on accelerated students. After all, based on the research, it is these students who experienced academic gains in tracked models.

When differentiation practices are fully implemented, they are used to expand the learning of accelerated students in the same way they support the learning of struggling students. Sometimes this means homogenous groupings are used within a heterogeneous classroom to allow accelerated students to work together. Sometimes it means extension work is assigned, the highest level of an assignment incorporates greater amounts of complexity, or lesson content is compacted and taught separately to this group so they can move more quickly. There is no singular differentiation strategy, but the idea that it is only effective for low-level students is an erroneous one.

Exposing our students on a daily basis to people who are different from them is perhaps the greatest society-changing influence schools can have. The biggest work is to guide students into becoming noble citizens; to do this, they must be provided with constant opportunities to see all the gifts (not just the academic ones) each individual in the classroom possesses. It is in these moments that students often experience the greatest growth and development. Not having these opportunities would be a tragic loss for all students—equally detrimental to our high-achieving students as to our struggling learners.

To address this, schools need more coteaching pairs, more opportunities for teaming and collaboration, more teacher training, and more resources that have valuable differentiation options embedded in them. In addition, teachers must push back against the message that every student should meet the same benchmark at the same time and replace it with the idea that every student must be pushed forward in their individual learning. This is accomplished through the work of differentiated instruction.

As educators, we are fundamentally charged with helping to level the playing field for our students, not contributing to the uphill battle. If we know tracked programming yields poor outcomes and potentially serves to maintain the racially linked economic disparity so prevalent in the United States, we simply must not do it.

Teachers and schools need to embrace differentiation, and coteaching as a best-practice strategy to support this work, as the means to meet the many needs of students. The work of differentiation is complex and challenging. There are as many ways to differentiate as there are classrooms. There is no single right way, and it may never be perfect, but in the absence of the elusive perfect strategy, teachers must embrace differentiation as a technique that is right for students. Teachers cannot tackle it all at once, but they must find a place to begin or grow.

TIPS OF THE TRADE

Differentiation Practices

- Begin slowly; identify the most crucial need for differentiation and start there.
- Remember that not every lesson or assignment needs to be differentiated.
- When planning for differentiation, begin with considering student needs and determine which of the following should be differentiated:
  - expectations
  - instruction
  - assignments
  - assessments
- Work to normalize differentiation in your classroom.
  - Intentionally vary groupings whenever possible.
  - Provide choice work, as well as leveled work.
  - Use language and grading practices that focus on growth rather than mastery.

    - Protect the confidentiality of leveled assignments by making assignments look as similar as possible and prelabeling assignments with students' names.
- Begin with three identified levels of differentiation or three choice options. As a teacher becomes more practiced with differentiation, this can be expanded to meet an even broader range of student needs.
- Identify assignment levels using positive language. Some options are:
    - emerging, practicing, extending
    - discovering, developing, adventuring
    - walking, jogging, running
    - wading, swimming, snorkeling
- Keep in mind this is challenging work. As difficulties arise, reflect and problem solve with colleagues to find creative solutions.

Coteaching Practices

- Don't try to go too fast; start with baby steps and then challenge yourselves to extend your practice.
- Coplan (this is crucial). It is not coteaching if you are not coplanning.
- Work with administration to establish common planning time for coteaching pairs.
- Present a united front.
    - Put both teachers' names on the door, on assignments, and in parent communication.
    - When referencing the class, identify both educators as the teachers.
    - Allow both teachers equal access to the electronic grade book, if possible.
    - Establish shared expectations and procedures.
- Share the load. This includes the following:
    - planning
    - creating materials
    - providing accommodations and modifications
    - grading
    - making parent phone calls
    - setting up the classroom
- When challenges present themselves, don't give up. Problem solve and make an adjustment in practice.

7

Using Real-World Experiences to Enhance Learning

Principal Duval was walking to a speaking engagement at the Westwood library when a car pulled into the driveway in front of him. Two young men stepped out. Both had been freshmen in his English class a couple years earlier, just before he had moved into administration.

The driver, Denson, was the type of student who would good-naturedly accept correction on his paper, before apologizing and committing to self-improvement after a teacher had pulled him aside to discuss his misbehavior in class; however, he would then, after an hour or a couple of days, continue right along making the same mistakes. Eventually, his course failures caught up to him, and he decided to drop out of school at the end of his junior year. At the time he left school, he could not articulate a plan to support himself or continue his education, despite the best efforts of the administration and team of teachers at the school.

On this day, Denson got out of the car and greeted Mr. Duval heartily. "I knew it was you!" he exclaimed, eagerly shaking his former teacher's hand. "I wanted to thank you, Mr. Duval," he added.

Mr. Duval was baffled. He could not determine why Denson would be thanking him. In that moment, and in the days following their encounter, Mr. Duval reflected on the ways he felt he had failed his student: the many parent or student conferences where teachers pointed out Denson's weaknesses without acknowledging his strengths, the fact that Denson left the school without earning a diploma, and how Mr. Duval had been unable to figure out how to keep him focused or help him see the importance of education.

Mr. Duval genuinely felt the gratitude was unwarranted. Denson's school experience had not, by many standards, been a success. But he was talking about more than a simple degree. Denson continued, "Mr. Duval, you guys never gave up on me, and you let me know I could be something once I put my mind to it. And now I am going to be a plumber. I never knew what I wanted to do until recently, but you guys said I could do it." He added, "Oh, and remember the song intersession? I think about that a lot. And white-water rafting? I wish school could have been like that all the time."

Denson's last comment demonstrates the powerful nature of experiential learning. Years after he left his formal education, he remembered positively two specific events. The songwriting intersession and a white-water rafting and mountain ecology intersession had created permanent memories for him and positive associations with school. Embedded in those experiences were lessons that included related readings, seminars, essay writing, and research. He successfully completed the kind of academic work in those events he found it difficult to complete during the rest of the school year. These activities kept him engaged and motivated, and he clearly required more of that than they could provide. The deepest learning he experienced happened outside the classroom.

THE PROBLEM

It is remarkable how little the standard classroom prepares students for the world of work. Even the office full of cubicles at a call center—the work environment that most resembles a traditional classroom—is seldom a place where everyone is doing the same thing at the same time

The Partnership for 21st-Century Learning, an influential and forward-thinking educational advocacy group helpful in structuring the 2015 Every Student Succeeds Act, supplements the antiquated "3 Rs" goals for successful schools. They point out that in addition to reading, writing, and arithmetic, students need life and career skills, learning innovation skills (which they call the "4 Cs"—critical thinking, communication, collaboration, and creativity), and information media and technology skills.

The reality is that a student who has learned to sit still for 45 minutes, move when a bell rings, answer multiple-choice questions, and solve only the odd-numbered math problems on the next page will be inadequately prepared for today's world.

This is a world where every part of their lives involves smart computers, working together to solve problems has replaced merely following orders, and disruptive technology might lead to a dozen career changes during a lifetime. Students need to be able to solve real problems that have direct consequences for them and others. Students need real-world experiences, and too many schools are giving them the exact opposite.

Today's teachers and principals remember escapes from the daily schedule from our own grade-school experience. The teacher announces, "We are going on a field trip next week," and sends home a permission slip. A bus is waiting on the appointed day, and teacher and students travel to a museum, a zoo, or some other attraction in a nearby city. We spend the day and return in time for dismissal. Over time, we as students remembered little other than the fact that we were out of the class, and that meant our spelling test was delayed for a day.

In most cases of the traditional field trip, after our return, we were unlikely to hear of the experience again, except when a teacher mentioned how much fun it was or how our misbehavior meant we might never leave the classroom, and certainly never for a field trip, ever again. Thus, the traditional field trip is a real-world experience of a sort, but a well-designed field *experience* can be so much more.

It is natural to want to place blame on students and hosts for this typical field-trip pattern, but it is irresponsible to do so. It is even possible that there was not actually "misbehavior," other than the fact that the students were being children in a place designed to host adults or closely supervised individuals. There are so many obstacles to creating real-world experiences for a class of students that it is a testament to teachers' resourcefulness that they happen at all. It is more likely that tradition is to blame. Described above is the prototypical field trip, as experienced by so many of us individually. A few of the obstacles to a successful field experience are as follows:

Limited budgets: The simplest trip can include a bus, entrance fees, and meals.

Limited time in the day: A typical school day is seven hours, but take away lunch, transitions, and setup and cleanup time, and add boarding and exiting buses and traveling, and one is left with perhaps only four hours of concentrated experience.

Limited time in the year: Most schools start with about 180 days; there is precious time left after removing time for essential classroom events, assemblies, pep rallies, fire and other mandated emergency drills, picture day, vision screenings, flu shots, and—don't forget—preparing for and taking the mandatory tests.

Limited space: Few places can take more than a handful of people at a time, so teachers often run into limitations on the number of students allowed or strict limitations on the adult–student ratio.

Student behavior (or misbehavior): It is no surprise that when students step into a new environment with unclear expectations, movement, and unusual spaces in which to stand or sit for unpredictable lengths of time, they become louder and more active.

Related concerns and obstacles: There may be few places to visit nearby, a lack of access to transportation, chaperones who are insufficient in number or temperament, and so on.

Despite these obstacles, it remains imperative that teachers prepare students for the world by providing experiential learning. This happens by first carving out field-experience time in the schedule and then making that time meaningful.

THE RESEARCH

The factory-model school, where a bell rings and students make their way through the conveyor belt of classrooms until they emerge "complete" on the other side, waving a diploma, is not the answer to the question of how to prepare today's students for tomorrow's world.

Historically, every time the United States has moved closer to education for everyone, the leaders of the time have spoken of the need to read philosophy and debate the great questions, make informed decisions, and participate in democracy by engaging in politics and casting reasoned votes. Our founders spoke of a great country ruled by an educated populace of individuals.

How times have changed. In 2015, Governor John Kasich of Ohio, planning for a run for the presidency, delivered a State of the State address that made it abundantly clear his vision of education is to use schools to teach industry-specific skills to create workers. "We must drive economic growth,"[1] he said, talking about the role of schools. This is a disheartening minimization of the value of a complete education, anathema to the full functioning of a democratic society.

The near-national adoption of the Common Core Standards, starting in 2009, and the standardized testing that has accompanied the implementation of No Child Left Behind have been the focus of vibrant debate. The controversial law contains widely popular goals, to be achieved by following a road map that has become rather unpopular, with 64% of respondents in one national poll saying "too much emphasis has been placed on testing."[2]

Substantial gains have been made in graduation rates in the United States from the low 60% range in the 1950s nationally.[3] In the state of Ohio, the graduation rate was 82.2% in 2013, according to Johns Hopkins University.[4] This has occurred with a bevy of changes, including reductions in class sizes, adoption of a national curriculum, and scorekeeping and school evaluation provisions of the No Child Left Behind Act. But while the attention to the need to increase the graduation rate is largely beneficial, there remains a wide range of descriptions of what a graduate should be able to do.

In this era of high-stakes testing and accountability, teachers require clarity about what "proficiency" looks like. And with school and teacher evaluations depending on standardized test scores, teachers are justifiably demanding that we minimize the number of interruptions and days out of the classroom. This pushes away even the most passionate educators from offering real-world experiences for their students.

The typical classroom, even the best-prepared one, is hardly equipped to prepare a child for whatever lies beyond high school (except, of course, if that child wants to become a teacher in a typical classroom). This is exacerbated by the misguided focus on standardized test scores, which force us to prepare kids for standardized tests—events most people never experience again after leaving school.

To keep students engaged and learning, we have to increase access to experiential learning opportunities. So, how do educators do that while protecting instructional time?

We must examine the child and understand that the deepest learning occurs outside of her seat and outside of the classroom's four walls. We must take her away from the school in reenvisioned field trips. These carefully constructed field experiences expose her to new situations and a variety of challenges. Only by venturing out into increasingly risky, widening gyres of activity and experience can she be fully prepared for what happens once she leaves the classroom after commencement.

THE SOLUTION: FIELD EXPERIENCES AND INTERSESSIONS

Few teachers or even principals are in a position to create an entirely new structure for education; they are confined to a certain calendar, and time constraints and requirements within these days. It is, after all, a structure that has endured for many generations and indeed crosses even cultural and national boundaries.

In high school, students must leave the classroom for most of the day and earn specific credits in other courses to be granted a diploma. This leaves students in dire need of experiences in actual businesses in a role other than customer, and in factories as someone other than a pedestrian on a sidewalk. Students need to see how the world works on the "other side of the glass;" they need to see what professionals see. And they need to do more than merely leave the classroom to fill a day in a teacher's syllabus. One way to address this need is through specialized and intentionally crafted field trips called "field experiences" and "intersessions."

Field experiences require more planning and intentionality than field trips. Field experiences are constructed by the teacher to support the learning objectives within a quarterly thematic unit or intentionally address an adolescent's need as they transition into a new community or seek greater independence. They are planned weeks or even months in advance, with time for reflection, observation, and deep practice of a skill, and with required work to be completed before, during, and after the experience.

This is as opposed to a field trip, which might start with a local amusement park offering a discounted rate for "math and science day" and a teacher interested in spending time with students outside of the classroom. Field experiences are intentional, experiential, related to the curriculum, and mandatory, while field trips are indeed experiential but may not relate to the curriculum and may even be optional.

Intersessions are expanded field experiences, intense courses of study that grant credit for specific learning. At the two public Montessori high schools in Cincinnati, these are immersive experiential learning periods that are not considered part of the academic quarter. About 10 days are "borrowed" from the middle of each semester, creating fall and spring intersessions.

> All high school students participate in intensive, academically rigorous field experiences called intersessions twice yearly, mid-semester. In the spring, students may choose from areas of study that include a wide variety of topics, from studying urban planning, infrastructure within our city, to exploring the biodiversity of the Great Smoky Mountains and the history of our nation's capital in Washington, DC. In the fall, students attend intersessions based on their class—for example, juniors focus on college preparation and take a college tour, while seniors participate in a career internship intersession.[5]

Denson's commentary on his school experience—which included whitewater rafting and writing and recording his own song—is evocative, and it is tempting to assert that real-life school experiences are the magic bullet for preventing dropouts and connecting a generation of students more powerfully with society; however, scant empirical evidence exists to support that claim. It is clear that these immersive experiences create powerful memories. This speaks to creating the connections upon which success can be built.

Imagine a curriculum where the student's day features trying new foods, setting challenging goals for himself, and building something he would not have otherwise known existed. This is the school one would wish for one's own child, is it not?

Teachers strive to find ways to make work unique for our students, seeking work that ignites a passion for learning. Students get choices in the topics they research or the books they read, because this ignition is what the students are seeking, too. Students seldom have real trouble concentrating on and learning about topics that engage their creativity, as well as their hands and minds.

It is through this kind of experience that we hope to help students achieve "flow." This is not just a slang word. The term *flow* is used by psychologist Mihaly Csikszentmihalyi to describe a sense of heightened engagement where an individual loses a sense of self and time.[6] It happens when the individual is being challenged at or just above the level of their skill. A student exploring a topic about which they want to learn more, sometimes being guided through this process of discovery by a skilled teacher, does not become "bored."

Teachers of adolescents are familiar with the struggle to keep them engaged and focused during a traditional 50-minute class, one of seven classes each day. We sympathize with the child who is unable to sit still and concentrate for that length of time, whose pubescent body wants to move and whose mind wants—and maybe needs—to wander. Keeping students in a state of flow throughout the day every day is not possible.

Through structuring unique experiences and challenges for students, we can increase their opportunities to experience this level of engagement. This "learner's high" is a desirable state, one that adolescents are naturally inclined to seek out, and if we can provide more of these experiences, the less we will have to deal with misbehavior during the time when students are not in "flow."

Dr. Maria Montessori describes every child as a natural learner, a student of the world. Whether it is Montessori's admonishment to "avoid the arrest of spontaneous movements and the imposition of arbitrary tasks"[7] or her proposal for the adolescent Erdkinder, where seventh and eighth graders (among those in what she calls the "third plane" of development, from ages 12 to 18) do real work, for example, raising crops and caring for livestock, that benefits the household, school, or community, a clear takeaway is that learning needs to be real and contribute not only to the education of the individual, but also whenever possible, be a productive part of society.

Teenagers have a special sensitivity to "arbitrary tasks," similar to their keen eye for authority figures' hypocrisy. Some teens will refuse to do work given seemingly just to fill time. Well-designed field experiences are the best opportunity to cut through their sensitivity, appeal to their desire for authenticity and belonging, and accomplish real work.

The Montessori concept of Erdkinder, child of the earth, speaks to the need of the adolescent to explore using all the senses. To climb, to pull, to dig, to plant, to reap, to collect, to categorize . . . adolescents are, each of them, a young Richard Byrd or Jane Goodall, pulled by a natural curiosity toward an unknown prize—a priceless treasure. Sometimes we forget this as we encourage them to finish their research paper or turn in their math homework, or we scold and hurry up the child touching her boots to the surface of a puddle.

There is no point in trying to change the nature of adolescents. In fact, their curiosity and malleability make the adolescent period the perfect time for education and the formation of moral code, acquisition of new languages, development of a healthy lifestyle and respect for one's body, and mastery of the basics of all academic disciplines. Of course, this is also the time to learn the rigors of scientific process and master the lifelong skill of dropping any once-favored theory that is contradicted by new, irrefutable evidence.

The Children and Nature Network, www.childrenandnature.org, has a long list of scholarly research that asserts the value of getting students into nature more often. Individual studies and meta-analysis of studies demonstrate positive correlations with school performance and learning, as well as physical health benefits, from regular exposure to nature. While some research suggests the benefit is heightened if the exposure happens weekly, periodic, in-depth camping and field experiences would appear to offer similar benefits.

Just as importantly, the research suggests a tangible benefit to being on a "real" field trip.[8] Students who experience learning in a real environment, whether on a nature trail or in a music studio, report learning more deeply and tend to remember the event longer. Also, the real location provides accurate and authentic details and feedback that cannot be imitated in any other setting. Thus, we struggle with how to give students work that is authentic or, better yet, give them real-world experiences.

Real-world experiences, however, can transform our sense of what is possible. They can uniquely open a student's eyes to the minutia and variety of life in a creek bed, for instance, not by showing a series of slides or re-creations, but by creating a memory of cold water running over the wrist as the hand submerges to overturn a stone, the stone splashing in the creek, and crayfish scarpering away, escaping in a cloud of silt. Or in the music studio, to turn the dials and have your friend's voice get louder or quieter, or deeper or higher pitched, or to stand on the carpeted floor and pluck a bass string and hear its sound resonate through the speakers, sounding different if you pluck with a pick or your finger.

In the real world, all the senses are open and attuned to an experience, and together they form a symphony of impulses that create memories to be recalled, even years in the future, by a sound or smell. D. A. Kolb's experiential learning theory states that ideas "are formed and reformed through experience."[9] We know this to be true from our personal experience and memories. Hence, it is crucial to give students real-world experiences. Yet, we can almost reflexively list the reasons it is so difficult to do. So, how do we pull this off? Like all great teachers, just take the available resources and get things done.

Ideally, every teacher wants to plan a field experience that is affordable (the perfect price is, of course, free) and aligned with their goals (preferably several strands in several different subjects). This should be an opportunity where the individuals who interact with our students are engaged and nurturing, and passionate about what they do, and where students work or learn in a way that is different from the manner in which they work or learn during typical instructional time. Oh, and we want a time in which our students behave like angels, just as we have instructed them.

Alas, teachers are not superheroes, and perfect is not going to happen. Perfect should not even be the goal. In fact, an experience with precise arrival and departure times, with students lined up in the correct order and everything happening without a hitch, conducted by a few precise and well-coordinated adults, deprives children of the opportunity to experience real-world problem solving. How can we model handling unexpected situations when we have planned them out of existence?

Likewise, too much uncertainty and too little planning can create anxiety and misbehavior, and turn your work into an expensive and angst-filled waste of time. There is a happy medium, somewhere closer to the "highly choreographed" end of the spectrum, where high-quality, real-life experiences can be structured for—and perhaps even *by*—each of your students.

Sincere interest and enthusiasm, more than technical skill and years of practice in the area, can create the best teacher, because passion ignites insatiable curiosity and desire for self-improvement. Instead of being merely a repository of information, like Google in human form, the teacher can and should learn and create alongside students in this process.

So, getting to a place is one challenge. What we find when we get there is another.

Teachers face a wide range of reactions and responses to having a group of adolescents out in public. Sometimes hosts will be welcoming and encouraging, and understand the work it takes to direct adolescents in the right way and take their foibles and oddities in stride. In other places, classes may encounter individuals who lack the understanding that teenagers in a new experience or space are often a little bit awkward, noisy, and experimental in their behavior. It is hard to predict exactly where each response will surface.

Even at such seemingly crowd- and student-friendly sites as science museums and zoos, teachers often run into individual employees who are not receptive to the visit or aware of the needs of teenagers. And while one might predict that the small farms, family businesses, or other small institutions where teachers take students for real-world learning experiences would be the least receptive to entertaining classes, it is there that some educators have found some of the most forgiving, welcoming, and patient hosts.

The teacher has an important role in preparing this environment, similar to the way he or she would prepare the classroom. Anticipating these situations and systematically planning for them helps create the optimal experience for students. And there are many practical examples.

In Rafe Esquith's book *Teach Like Your Hair's on Fire*, the author proposes an intentional solution: Teach students the expected behavior, practice it, and remind them and enforce it on location.[10] He proposes teaching students how to sit on an airplane, for example. This is the perfect approach.

Take the time in advance to anticipate and teach how to handle certain obstacles you will encounter in the real world. That means entrusting students to make plans for specific details and events throughout the field experience. While a past generation of teachers may have given the instruction, "Grab a buddy's hand," that is clearly insufficient for explaining to students how they should behave at the natural history museum, where there are exhibits that can be touched or items that can be lifted and shared.

Plan for this. Teach the skills, practice the actions. Set aside time to explain how the airport works, teach the travel axiom "hurry up and wait," role play how to go through security at the courthouse, or ask students to plan tent groups weeks in advance of the camping trip. Invest an afternoon in advance of fall camp simply setting up and tearing down tents until everyone is comfortable with the process and the pieces. Leave little to chance. Life will provide its own surprises, and these prepared students will make a plan for exactly how to proceed.

Specialized preparation is needed for a portion of the trip to Pigeon Key, Florida, taken annually at one school. While most of the experience is spent on an isolated marine biology outpost on an island not much larger than a couple of football fields, teachers and students used to take a day trip to Key West as part of the cultural experience.

Like other beach vacation spots, the Key West tourist shopping experience includes exposure to profanity on souvenirs, public consumption of alcohol and drunkenness, and lewd T-shirts, posters, and wall hangings. Key West, in particular, could expose students to inappropriate comments from tourists, sex toys in stores, drag queens, and same-sex public displays of affection. Students would naturally be curious about these things, and since they are teenagers, the one thing one could predict is that their reactions would be unpredictable.

Rather than leave the situation and response up to chance, teachers present these possibilities to the group of students in advance, provide a conceptual understanding of what they are likely to encounter, and give appropriate responses. (This does *not* mean bringing examples to school, of course. Thoughtful preparation for exposure to inappropriate items is a professional responsibility of a teacher. Intentional exposure to something inappropriate as "preparation" for the possibility of exposure is unacceptable and an abrogation of the teacher's deepest responsibility to the child.)

Some may argue that this planning undermines the idea of experiential learning. "If you plan for all of these things," the reasoning goes, "then students will never encounter real problems." Oh, how teachers wish this was true. Real life will unfailingly present new challenges. Eliminating variables so that students are comfortable with much of what is going on makes it easier to solve new problems that arise.

For instance, being comfortable with setting a tent up in good conditions makes it possible to do the same in difficult circumstances, say, in the rain. This increases the students' likelihood of success, and builds the students' self-efficacy. In the songwriting intersession that Denson recalled, leaving little to chance meant making specific plans for how the group would go to a fast-food restaurant for a quick lunch, keeping in mind healthy options. They reviewed their orders on the walk over. There was little opportunity for misbehavior because the group walked in with a plan.

Owing, in part, to teachers' collective effort to expand student horizons beyond those imagined by their parents, and perhaps more largely to the engagement of students' creativity and interest, you will find these experiences have nearly perfect attendance. They certainly create stronger memories and provide a wide range of useful skills beyond those called for in the Common Core Standards.

"Ms. Rachel!" called a voice from the telephone. "You know I like you, and I think this is a great field-trip idea, but you just can't expect my daughter to catch a new bus to Clifton!"

On the first day of her intersession, one of the parents in Ms. Rachel's intersession determined to keep her daughter safe by bringing her—about an hour tardy—to the library at the University of Cincinnati before she went to work. To make matters worse, Mom's choice to drop off her daughter instead of helping her ride the bus made Mom late to work and mad at the teacher.

Ms. Rachel believed, correctly, that this student (like most high school students) was capable of making the trip, but she was not willing or able to take a strong position with her mother without first doing some groundwork. Thus, on the afternoon of the first day, she met with the student and they planned out the route for the next morning. The student sat beside Ms. Rachel as she called her mother to share the plan, which gave the student greater independence and autonomy than she had before. Ms. Rachel also got an opportunity to exhibit grace and courtesy, as the mother used that phone call as an opportunity to complain about being late to work. Ms. Rachel surmised that this was the wrong time to point out that if she had brought her daughter to the library on time, she likely would have made it to work on time, too.

During the conversation detailing the plans Ms. Rachel and the student had made together, it was clear from the student's body language that she was uncomfortable having this conversation with her mother or that Ms. Rachel was having it. She had learned that her mother's rules were final. This is a great lesson for a seven-year-old to learn, but a 15-year-old is in a different place developmentally. She needed to gain confidence and the language of self-advocacy.

Before the call, Ms. Rachel and the student were able to plan the part of the route where the student would meet up with a classmate at a major stop in town. From there she would text her mother, and she would do this again when she reached the library. The plan worked as scheduled for the rest of the intersession. She was on time for most of the remaining days. More importantly, mother and daughter had established a new structure for interacting with one another, with the student being better equipped to take initiative and be an advocate for herself, and the parent gaining new confidence in her child's decision-making and planning skills.

One of Mr. Duval's students remembers intersession as follows:

> I really enjoyed learning about GarageBand and attempting to make my own song. I loved that we had one big project that we worked on the whole time and then smaller song projects based on certain types of music during the week. This allowed us to practice and mess around with sound we would not have experimented with otherwise.
>
> It was cool to watch other people use the microphone or play their own instruments to incorporate their own style into the song. The experience at the studio was awesome. I had never been to a studio before, so I was just in awe. I enjoyed seeing all the aspects of the studio: sitting in the control room and watching everyone, and being in the live room. Everyone was able to play an instrument or sing, and it was recorded. . . . Everyone was on beat, and the song ended up sounding pretty good, and it was funny!
>
> This was definitely one of my favorite intersessions of my high school career.

It is revealing that so much of the student's memory focuses on two things: the product she was asked to create—her own song—and the time spent in the recording studio. The first was the "big work" in which the most time was invested during the two weeks. The second was a half-day spent in the most authentic music-making setting.

It makes clear that authentic learning involves doing real work in the same place that the work is always done and creating something of your own. The student took risks, tried new things, and was shown ways to expand her horizons not available in a typical classroom.

Through perseverance, planning, and admirable student tolerance, Mr. Duval was able to put together a memorable and educational intersession on songwriting. In this real-life experience, students learned the recording program GarageBand and created a song—either individually or with a partner—according to the qualifications he provided, and the songs appeared on a compilation CD. A copy of this CD, with a collage of the artwork each student produced to accompany their song, was given to each student as a keepsake. Some students have reported keeping this CD with their collection to this day.

How is this a "real-life" experience? In several ways. First, students worked directly with the same tools recording artists use, as GarageBand has been used by well-known artists to create popular music. Second, students got a chance to use instruments, microphones, and other tools in a recording studio. Although there were some exercises to lead them to explore the functions in GarageBand, there were few restrictions on their final product. There is no wrong way to write a song. The range of final songs were as varied as the individuals in the room.

Third, students were involved in problem solving with one another. They had ample time each day to work on their own projects and cocreate. Organic conversations arose when students shared clips of their work and taught one another how to layer and clip sounds, create loops, and make existing GarageBand sounds in unique ways. "Real life" is just that—organic learning and sharing in an environment built for that type of activity.

Our experience was not perfect or perfectly planned. Mr. Duval's biggest regret was not holding a meaningful final ceremony. Had he planned better, he laments, a listening party would have been the culminating activity. Together as a group, with snacks and a nice stereo, they could have listened to the songs, with each artist introducing the song, describing what was learned throughout the process, and guiding the audience in what to listen for.

As it was, as students walked into class several days after the intersession ended, and Mr. Duval handed them their own copy of the CD, a collection of each of their songs, with "skits" in between—moments taken from their time with the mics open and recording at the studio. This final totem provided students with an object onto which they could focus their positive memories and success.

So, how can a teacher overcome the many obstacles that arise in planning an experience, whether it is one day or day 10? Ultimately, we are only limited by our imagination, planning, and capacity to respond to a situation with optimism. Two students remember with fondness a field experience from years earlier, because of the opportunity to use authentic tools in the act of creating something novel. There is a depth of learning and remembering that cannot be matched in the classroom.

The aforementioned problems—limited time, budgets, and space, along with student misbehavior and various expectations and skill sets of the host venue—are faced by all teachers as they plan their field trips, intersessions, and field experiences. These problems, in one form or another, come up again and again. They can crop up even as teachers plan recurring events at educational attractions that have worked with their students before.

Guide problems: Your guide, often a volunteer, can make or break your visit. Even a welcoming site like the local natural history museum is really only as proficient as the individual classroom guide assigned to the group on a given day.

Look but don't touch problems: Owners of businesses might be tempted to act much like a museum curator, inviting students to look but not touch as they tour a work site.

Price points: Expensive trips require the same fund-raising effort each year, as a new round of students arrive.

Teachers have found many inventive ways to solve the problems that are part and parcel of creating an experience. The following are some solutions. This is not an exhaustive list, but instead a resource as the reader encounters some of these same issues.

CONCLUSION

At the beginning of the chapter, Denson pulls his car over and wants to discuss his memories of school, especially the positive impressions he gained during his intersessions. Field experiences and intersession did not transform Denson as a student, nor did they provide sufficient impetus for him to begin regularly completing homework and engaging in the work and learning happening in class; however, there is something to be gained from simply contrasting his recollections of school with those of other unsuccessful students.

There are many individuals whose experiences in school were uniformly negative or whose predominant memory of schooling or a particular teacher is filled with loathing and anger. Sometimes this even occurs with students who were successful in school, earning good grades and a diploma.

Every school has students like Denson who yearn for meaningful work. These students should be engaged through active learning connected to the standards and larger thematic ideas within each discipline and the school.

Educators have to find a way for all students to experience success and engagement, so that they can experience a wider array of opportunities. The best answer to the problem of student disengagement and rejection of inauthentic learning is to construct and implement regular field experiences and intersessions to provide intentional engagement of the mind, body, and spirit.

TIPS OF THE TRADE

How can a teacher plan and implement a field experience? Most teachers are able to get the support necessary to take a group of students out of the building for a day or a few hours in support of learning goals. The following are some things to consider when planning and implementing your trip.

Curricular Imperative

- Thinking about your unit plan, upcoming assignments, and the curriculum, create an experience that allows for hands-on learning relevant to your desired outcomes. Tie it to the following:
  - Common Core Standards
    - School core values, mission, and vision
    - Service and connection to the community
    - The needs of the adolescent seeking autonomy
  - Prework and postwork, for instance, presentations, that emphasize the connection of the experience to the curriculum

Budget and Finances

- Use available resources as much as possible.
  - Meet at and dismiss from the school during school hours.
  - Provide bag lunches from the school cafeteria.
  - Use spaces in the school or other schools and public places.
  - Carpool.
  - Ask for discounts at educational sites.
  - Ask friends for related resources.

Use of Time in the Day

- Use a block schedule or set aside entire days.
- Have meetings and professional development outside of the scheduled day to free up instructional time.
- Develop systems in the classroom to capture transitional time.

Managing and Planning for Student Behavior

- Teach expectations for each type of site you will visit.
- Plan for "downtime" where students can relax and not have to be on their best "museum" behavior.
- Build multiple reminders into the schedule and support work (verbal and in writing).

Use of Time in the Year

- Plan overnight or weekend events.
- Intentionally schedule testing to limit time lost.
- Have summer bridge or other student or parent orientation events outside of the school day.

Use of Space

- Use common spaces in the school (e.g., auditorium, gym, cafeteria, large classrooms, outdoor spaces).
- Use other public and private buildings (e.g., nearby schools, libraries, and churches).

Preparing Hosts and Host Sites

- Let sites know your group's activity level.
- Meet with host site in advance to determine their rules and expectations.
- Request a current or former teacher as your liaison, if available.
- Share with the host site your rules and expectations, and what you have taught students about their behavior while at the site (including plans for downtime).

8

Practicing What You Preach: Using Modeling to Effect Real Change

Humbled and honored by his peers who supported his move from teaching into administration, not just anywhere, but at their same school, Tom found himself feeling suddenly alone and vulnerable in the days after signing the administrative contract. He knew he could do the work. He loved the school even more deeply than he had thought possible. He was in the right place. Almost nothing had changed.

But everything had changed.

He realized his responsibilities and even his loyalties were different in important ways. If his teaching partner from last year were to share a joke about another teacher in the school, he could no longer laugh. It was now his job to foster unity and protect information about his employees. Each of them had strengths, weaknesses, and blind spots, and each of them contributed meaningfully to the whole. If he laughed about one behind their back, would anyone trust ever him again?

He knew the answer was "no."

Years of teaching had given Tom some of the tools he would need to be principal, but not all, and he would have to wield them differently. He found himself receiving advice and accolades, surrounded by well-wishers and coworkers almost constantly. Yet, he found himself alone.

The feeling was amplified the day he signed his first administrative contract with the district. He walked into the main office in human resources and was ushered into an executive suite, through a door he had only ever seen closed. The human resources director greeted him politely and pulled a paper from a folder on the desk.

"Good to see you, Tom. Now if you will just sign there," he said, pointing to a signature line at the bottom of the page.

Tom signed.

"Ok, well that was all we needed." The director scooped up the paper and deftly returned it to the folder, as if he had done it dozens of times, as if perhaps a hundred or more different times someone had come into that office to completely upend their career.

"I, uh," Tom stammered, shocked by the brevity of the interaction. "There's no orientation? I mean, maybe a binder of policies or a principal handbook or something?"

The director paused, understanding the request. He stepped around the table, stood up straight, and offered his right hand. Tom shook it. "Welcome to administration. Good luck!"

Leadership is challenging and can be lonely. Even teachers, imbued by society with an assumed moral authority, who can lead a classroom of students, struggle in leading adults. Incrementally, they learn the ropes of leading students instead of merely bossing them around. Then they step into teacher leadership roles, as committee leaders, department chairs, program facilitators, or some other title, and learn some more. And yet, sometimes they still find it almost impossible to talk openly with a colleague who they think handled a situation poorly.

The only thing harder than addressing someone's misstep when you have authority over them is addressing the misstep when you work closely with them but have no perceived situational authority.

Worse, there is an overabundance of leadership books, videos, and other resources to guide the aspiring leader. Many are written for the business world and can have a different conscience than educational leadership books. It would be impossible to read them all and equally difficult to implement the advice they provide, especially since the details can be dramatically contradictory.

Whether you hope to be principal or simply want to work with others who share your passion for improving their teaching, there are concrete skills you can master to have the kinds of conversations and create the kind of professional development that inspires passion and improvement in an entire school.

THE PROBLEM

Teaching is a demanding job. First, teachers see a lot of people on a daily basis; as many as 150 students may pass through a single high school classroom during the course of a day. Students are there for 50 or—if one has the blessing of having block schedules—100 minutes until the bell rings, and then they are replaced by another set of students. In the elementary classroom, these days are longer, allowing for more natural relationships to form; however, even these rich interactions are shaped by an annual calendar instead of a natural cycle.

Even elementary teachers, blessed (or, some may joke, cursed) with extended time with a small group of students, find that the beginning of the year comes far too quickly on the heels of summer and the end of the year and concomitant ending of these relationships can be painfully abrupt. Deep investments made building students' skills and habits walk out the door in June, with large questions unanswered. Making it to the end of the calendar in education is not necessarily the same as reaching a goal.

In addition to the pace of these interactions and the transience of the relationships comes the overwhelming volume of decisions. A recent Gallup poll indicates that 46% of teachers experience high levels of daily stress. It is at the top of surveyed professions and puts teachers in a category similar to nurses.[1]

In addition to the myriad complex interactions with students, peer relationships are challenging for teachers, too. For most of the day, teachers cannot work directly together, but instead must work parallel to one another. Many schools offer such structures as teams and departments to provide professional support, but often these structures are used by teachers to do the indirect work of preparing for teaching or solving problems after an issue has arisen, or even prescriptive professional development, but not the actual practice of teaching.

Teachers, like other workers, can also feel as if their boss does not understand what the work entails. Hence, they are often left feeling as if they must lead themselves either individually or by creating informal leadership roles for themselves as a group. A common example is the teacher who becomes the de facto "tech person" for the team. She might not have any additional training on technology, but her interest and enthusiasm allow her to work in a supportive role with her peers, and she is given high esteem for this.

More formally, teachers may be tapped to lead professional development. Armed with years of classroom management and presumed authority over students, they find themselves responsible for working with or training adults who may—or may not—be fully invested in the training. Yet, these teacher leaders are the best resource for gaining the skills and insight they need. Sometimes they have precisely the information a teacher needs to work past a complex problem. Aside from giving advice on how to get students to turn in their homework, another teacher might know why a given student was uncharacteristically morose and unresponsive in class on a given day. Communication and instruction between teachers can make or break individual student relationships and an entire school year.

Leadership of peers requires a different set of skills than classroom management. This is one of the sources of loneliness felt by Tom in the previous anecdote.

THE RESEARCH

According to one account, teachers make approximately 1,500 work-related decisions a day—about four per minute during their six hours with students. This is on top of the almost 35,000 decisions adults make throughout the span of a day, including the more than 200 made about food alone.[2] Sure, these are not all life-and-death decisions, but the energy drained by pondering each question is real.

Teachers are frequently asked to step up into leadership roles, and many want to do so, but the demands on time are great. Organization, discipline, and hard work are requisite characteristics of teacher leaders, who must cope with the stress of teaching, while making a time and space in their schedule for supporting their coworkers.

Recent comprehensive studies show that new teacher attrition is at an alarming 17% after five years,[3] with some estimates placing it as high as 50%. Thus, one might think this is an existential crisis for education. Yet, the number of teachers staying until retirement in education is also high. This demonstrates that while some new teachers struggle to learn the job, there are many individuals who persist, endure, and even thrive in this career, seeing it through until they reach an age where they can comfortably move into retirement.

These veteran teachers, then, can be a gold mine. Capturing the essence, energy, and tips and tricks of successful and energetic experienced teachers is an obvious way to promote longevity and skill-building among new teachers. Passing these skills and this enthusiasm on to younger teachers is not merely a good idea, it is the answer to creating a thriving school culture.

But there are limitations to the amount of work that can be taken on, even by these veterans. Already overworked and stressed, teachers are not always able to provide the leadership required by new teachers at the necessary level of intensity.

Administrators are the obvious answer for providing support, but teachers tend to feel unsupported by their administrative staff. In a recent survey at Cult of Pedagogy, a popular teaching blog, one respondent complained, "I have far more education and teaching experience than my principal. She is threatened by my expertise and openly hostile to hearing opinions that are different from hers."[4] So, how does an administrator provide effective supports without risking alienating new teachers who are striving to be successful and independent?

Principals clearly have an important role to play in improving the experience of new teachers. Involving new teachers in communication and decision-making is empowering, and helps keep teachers in the profession.[5] Efforts to train, promote, and involve teachers are a necessary part of an administrator's work, but even this is not enough by itself.

Moreover, administrators have an important role to play in quelling the voices of the negative veterans who see the work as a series of necessary chores to pass the time until the next weekend—and the next paycheck. Careful cultivation of leadership in the building through intentional promotions and pairings is work that only an administrator can do. It takes an "all of the above" approach to prevent the work of teaching from backsliding into just another job. The most successful teams of teachers will provide mentorship, skill-building, and involvement in the school. On these teams, a most important aspect is the ability of teachers and administrators to model the change they want to see in others.

THE SOLUTION

Teacher Leadership

Teachers and principals must accept responsibility for changing themselves and be open to that change. Organizations and societies do not simply reform themselves to meet the needs of those who merely vocalize complaints. In fact, teachers, principals, and everyone in the school setting tend to present what Robert Kegan and Lisa Laskow Lahey call an "immunity to change," where they unconsciously try to preserve the status quo, even if they are outwardly unhappy with it.

Kegan asserts that "collectivities—work teams, leadership groups, departmental units, whole organizations—also unknowingly protect themselves from making the very changes they most desire."[6] It is precisely this tendency in groups, and individuals, that leaders must learn to defend against. Even the most sought-after change a person wants to make in themselves, for example, losing weight or getting more sleep, is subject to a fierce defense from forces inside the person hoping to make the change.

The response is to understand that the most important change one can make is a change within oneself. Teachers who wish to change their classroom or school, or even effect a specific change in the habits and practices of an individual student, must determine their place in the current set of habits and make intentional change.

Teachers tell their students every day to be ready, willing, and able to change themselves. This act of self-reinvention is scary, and the teacher must be willing to lead and model this change. We must empower one another to get better at what we do.

The day before winter break, one teacher found herself pacing back and forth in the hallway outside of Steve's classroom just before first bell, trying to muster up the courage to go in. She didn't do it. She returned during his planning bell and at lunch but could not have the intended conversation.

The night before, she had resolved to have a difficult conversation.

A few days earlier, she had popped into Steve's classroom to ask a question, but in the brief time there, she observed students in this class violating several basic building-wide expectations. When she corrected the students, they indicated they were allowed to do these things in Steve's class.

This bothered her, not because the students' behavior was particularly disruptive. It wasn't. (The rule-breaking in question was about dress code, headphones, and the food and drink policy.) But the building-wide expectations were supposed to be "building-wide." She had enforced them in her own classroom, sometimes creating conflict, but also creating a sense of clear, shared expectations and values.

It would have been easy to just ignore it. Ignoring it was especially tempting because Steve was a kind and helpful teacher, and a friend. Ignoring it was easy. In any case, correcting a fellow teacher isn't even a teacher's job, is it? Isn't that the work of an administrator? Coworkers have no obligation to hold one another accountable for expectations, at least in a traditional, top-down view of the workplace.

This was the argument she had tried to hide behind for days, but it wasn't sitting properly. What was being helped by being privately irritated by the actions of someone she liked and respected? What was being helped by not addressing concerns directly? By failing to do so, she was potentially setting up her friend and colleague to be corrected by an administrator. How was that helpful to him?

Teachers understand the unique needs, challenges, and fears of the profession in a way no one else can. Who better to offer advice and support to a teacher than a teacher? Who better to offer correction and redirection? A peer can offer advice without it being evaluative. A peer can offer advice from the perspective of having the same demands on their own time and energy. A trusted peer can listen to fears and flaws without judgment and help balance the stresses of personal and professional life. There are many formal and informal ways for teachers to step up and provide for one another the leadership needed in any situation.

One way to do this is to seek informal mentors.

One teacher, wary of placing additional stress on others and not wanting to be seen as bothersome for asking too many questions, "adopted" a set of informal mentors. If she saw someone who had a strength in organization, she observed them closely, sometimes asking specific questions about their rationale for doing things a certain way, while other times merely co-opting a certain structure or behavior that seemed effective.

Another teacher, struggling with the weight of the many roles he had taken on in the school, went to the principal to ask for advice on being organized. This particular tactic, seeking out mentorship from other leaders, including administration, can serve multiple purposes. First, it alerts administration to the teacher's desire for self-improvement. Second, the leader likely has some good advice on managing tasks and work, which can be incorporated to lighten the burden. Third, it allows for informal conversations to reveal which work is most valued and build the relationships that help form any successful community.

Another way for teachers to provide this leadership is to intentionally mentor others. Draw one person under your wing by letting them know you are available for questions, asking direct questions about specific aspects of the work and getting involved in their teaching. Perhaps more importantly, offer to help with a specific task. Are they grading an assignment? Offer to do half. Share a rubric or procedure for how this work gets handled efficiently in another classroom.

Teacher Mentoring at Gamble Montessori

One teacher leader strongly advocated creating a mentoring process that would do three things: provide guidance on the basic pieces of working in the building, assist with understanding the processes used for handling a variety of situations, and include a deep sharing of the school culture.

After weeks of discussing potential approaches to this work and looking for viable models for how to do it, school representatives met with Brian Cundiff, executive vice president of operations at LaRosa's, a prominent local pizza chain, to discuss their "onboarding" process. LaRosa's makes pizza. Gamble Montessori educates children. What could possibly be learned? As it turns out, a lot.

LaRosa's had developed a thoughtful process for ensuring that every employee understood what the company was about. A number of statements stood out during the meeting. Mr. Cundiff emphasized that the employer has a responsibility to grow team members and that there is need to train every person in the system to ensure maintenance of the culture you are trying to establish. Additionally, the best teachers are peers. The person taking orders at the table next to you is able to provide support, modeling, and even polite correction in a way that a manager cannot. Finally, to articulate what needs to be communicated about your culture, look back at your vision statement and be a storyteller.

Their program included three layers that are important for not only determining a process for getting things done at school, but also helping create and pass on the culture of the school. An overview of expectations and procedures is covered in their preorientation requirements—essentially a reading of the staff manual. Following the preorientation, instructions for how to handle a variety of situations are given during an in-person orientation session. But the most important thing Mr. Cundiff shared was the importance they placed on sharing the Buddy LaRosa story with every employee and every customer. This is the story every new employee hears:

> As people traveled to Buddy's original pizzeria to satisfy their hunger, sharing pizza, smiles, and stories together, he quickly saw that the more his guests smiled, the more often they came back. As his business grew, Buddy began to realize that the making smiles part was the most important work he did—LaRosa's reason to exist. "Reach Out and Make Smiles" was born soon thereafter as Buddy's service philosophy.

This philosophy is summarized and displayed on pizza paddles in every restaurant. It goes beyond pizza; it explains who they are, at their heart.

During the summer before the 2014–2015 school year, using what had been gleaned from LaRosa's, the Teacher:Teacher mentoring program at

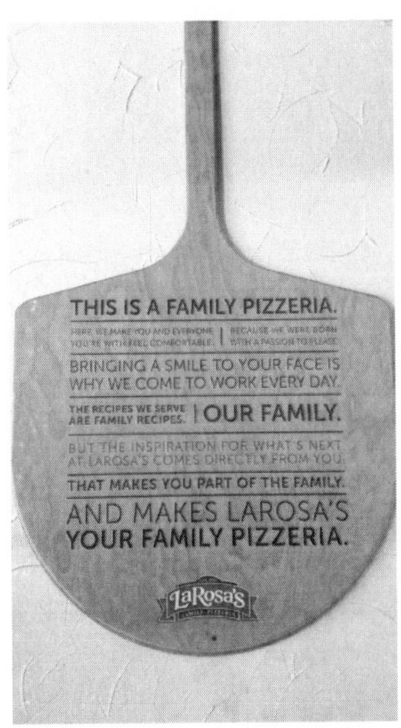

FIGURE 8.1
Buddy LaRosa's Service Philosophy on a Pizza Paddle

Gamble was piloted. Still in regular use, there are important key features that should be part of any mentoring program. New teachers are paired with carefully selected veteran teachers, allowing for a high level of consistent support provided by a reliable and knowledgeable peer. A booklet is provided to each new teacher to serve as an overview of the basics. Most importantly, it includes a checklist of important things for mentors to cover with mentees before school even starts, including such crucial components as a building tour (including the location of the cafeteria), where to sign in, and even details on how to use the copier.

Monthly meetings cover Montessori philosophy, the state evaluation system, and testing protocols, among many other things. These meetings also provide a time to ask questions; provide feedback on the program; and meet with key school personnel to answer questions about how the technology functions, how the student schedule works, and other issues of interest to new teachers.

Finally, scheduled one-on-one check-ins between mentor and mentee allow for the pair to problem-solve concerns and the veteran to provide encouragement and support. Making this the intentional work of a selected volunteer mentor and intentionally setting aside time for this work means that a new teacher does not have to feel as if they are imposing when they ask a question that is complicated to answer. It removes the stigma of being the one who asks too many questions or the feeling of responsibility for having "wasted" someone else's time. This is time well spent.

PLCs

At every school, there are additional ways for teachers to take on leadership with or without the support of administration or the creation of a mentoring program. School teams regularly form professional learning communities, or PLCs, as described for dozens of years by Richard DuFour. This can take on a variety of forms and be called many different things, for example, a 90-day plan or a turnaround plan, and be incorporated in personal or professional growth plans, school One Plans, or nationally required improvement plans associated with Title I grants.

Whatever it is called, the true goal of a PLC is to identify a common problem directly related to student learning and solve it as a team. The process is exhaustively described in other resources, but it merits a quick summary here.

The team identifies an area related to student learning outcomes where the results are poor or inconsistent with other scores throughout the building or some larger area, or simply could be better. This is often related to standardized test scores but could relate to other areas, for instance, living up to the school's core values or such visible indicators of academic success as grades. Then the team drills down to find the details of the identified problem. What is it, exactly, that is providing the suboptimal results?

Armed with this data, the team takes a key next step: conducting research. This is where PLCs differ from typical team solutions. Oftentimes teams of teachers get together to solve a problem and the depth of their knowledge comes from their own experience; however, even the most veteran teacher finds his or her knowledge limited by his or her own narrow scope of professional experience. Seeking outside sources for ideas, including books, scholarly articles in professional publications, and even teaching blogs by teachers in the same subject or age band, allows the team to discuss and evaluate a wide array of possible solutions.

Armed with new knowledge, the team can review possibilities and decide on a way forward. They can collectively implement the plan for the indicated period of time. This typically provides for a midyear check-in to evaluate progress and an end-of-year final review.

If the intervention worked, the team should keep it and add it to their repertoire. Team members may even seek to apply this approach to other subjects, classes, or situations if it is readily transferrable.

Or maybe the team does not solve anything. Maybe the data reveals they did not impact the problem. This is information, too. Sometimes the strategy the team believed was most likely to impact the problem has no effect. This is also data, and "no effect" is not failure. The only failure is not trying something different to impact the outcome.

Teams that use the PLC approach do not solve all of their problems at once. They do, however, solve their most pressing problem. More importantly, perhaps, they solve the problem together and build capacity and resources for solving future problems together. This provides a rich and satisfying work experience and improves outcomes.

Individual or Paired Skill-Building

Another way teachers can gain the competencies they need to feel successful is through individual or paired skill-building and self-study. One principal saw a presentation by Craig Weber, author of *Conversational Capacity: The Secret to Building Successful Teams That Perform When the Pressure Is On*. He found the presentation eye-opening. Knowing that a teacher in his building was intentionally seeking out ways to develop herself professionally, he suggested they read the book together. They carved out time to read the book, discuss it, and implement the ideas.

Craig's premise is that the critical factor for teams is not the much-touted establishment of trust and respect. Rather, it is the development of "conversational capacity"—or, as he describes it, the "ability to have open, balanced, nondefensive dialogue about tough subjects and in challenging circumstances."

He describes this as being in the conversational "sweet spot"—that place in a conversation or meeting where candor and curiosity are in balance. But he also cautions that while this sounds deceptively simple, our human nature tends to get in the way of our ability to remain in this balanced place when facing pressure or discussing challenging issues. "While it's easy to remain balanced when talking about routine and comfortable issues, when a difficult subject hits the table, our tendency is to move out of the sweet spot toward the extreme ends of the behavioral spectrum. Some people shut down. Others heat up."[7]

Principal and lead teacher worked on these ideas together during the course of the year, applying the ideas to specific situations in the building and thinking about how to change their own practices to match the advice in the book. There were mixed results, as happens in the implementation of new practices and the development of new skills. The important part was that they were engaged in a professional practice of intentional improvement.

Voluntary Small-Group Piloting

Teachers can also enhance their professional skills through voluntary piloting of practices. One teacher learned she and another teacher at her school were both independently trying to improve practices concerning differentiated learning. They speculated that others might be trying to do the same thing, so they reached out to others in the school, inviting them to an organizational meeting early in the year.

Originally, there were 10 of them, but after this first meeting, they were reduced to just seven through self-selection. Initially, the small number of participants was disappointing. Where were the hordes of teachers flocking together to improve their practice? But in hindsight, the small group size may have been one of the key components of their success. The pilot program was purely voluntary, and this ensured that only people willing to commit to doing the work in a positive and forward-thinking way joined the group.

This meant that while they didn't have the anticipated number of members, they also didn't have the uncommitted, disengaged participants that can derail even the most well-thought-out professional development. Because the group was made up of volunteers, they were free to develop the work into whatever it was they thought would work for them. Although they were teachers in the same building, they represented a variety of grade levels and departments—seventh and eighth grade, 11th and 12th grade, social studies, language arts, math, science, special education, and music.

It is important in any voluntary pilot group to develop clear expectations of the work. The parameters a voluntary group should establish include meeting frequency and duration; a specific academic focus; and a willingness to share in the work, both through examination of artifacts and classroom observations (or "friendly feedback observations").

During the second meeting, this particular group shared their successes and challenges, quickly discovering they were already doing a lot. Simply stating differentiation as an intention at their initial meeting in September had motivated each of them to work toward furthering their practice in this area. Some reported success at small inroads: providing read-aloud options on a more consistent basis, using a wider variety of instructional groupings, or allowing students with prior piano experience to branch out into guitar exploration during music class.

Some of the independent successes were quite significant: providing weekly checklists/work plans that were uniquely tailored to students' needs or individualizing assessments such that each student received different questions on a physics test.

The group had their share of noteworthy challenges as well, and they still had a long way to go to develop what they wanted to see in their classrooms. The group narrowed their focus based on the early work. Group members noted that their challenges clustered into four areas: differentiation of assessments, differentiation of assignments, differentiation of instruction, and differentiation of expectations. They quickly realized they were putting the cart before the horse by starting with the products (the assessments and assignments) rather than the students (the expectations). Being a small, flexible group, members were able to shift their practice and get the focus in the right place.

A voluntary piloting group should also work to celebrate successes together and take a hard look at common challenges. Halfway through the first year, this particular group remained dissatisfied with the number of students earning failing grades despite their structures and supports. How could this be? They had worked so hard. How could their efforts still have not been enough to support students? Members examined their practices, continued to make changes, and persisted.

Being in a voluntary piloting group with like-minded professionals also allows for honest feedback. This particular group recognized it felt uncomfortable with meeting students where they were and moving them forward along a continuum, even if they didn't ultimately reach the grade-level outcome. Their mandate as teachers is to get students to "proficient" by the end of the year, no matter where these students were when they arrived. Hence, group members brought in expert educators to provide solace and encouragement they were heading in the right direction.

One particularly profound discussion occurred when the argument was made that a teacher can't give an excellent grade to a student who has not met the intended standard by the end of the year. A wise veteran teacher asked a question about those students whose skills were so low when they entered that a year's worth of growth did not get them to the passing mark. She asked about these theoretical students, "Are they learning?"

The answer was a resounding "yes."

Her response shifted the entire conversation and convinced the members they were on the right path: "How can they be failing if they are learning?"

The group committed to helping students learn as much as possible, without ever labeling growth as failure. At the end of the year, voluntary piloting did not result in 100% student mastery of grade-level material; however, much was accomplished. This small group of educators improved their practice and demonstrably moved students toward successful completion of their classes.

The goal is not to find all the answers to the selected problems. The goal is to strengthen teaching practices and help students and teachers increase their skills in areas of need. Voluntary piloting promotes and supports this work, without the involvement of anyone other than interested teachers.

So, voluntary piloting provides a unique and supportive environment in which to try new approaches to important problems, without the involvement of the administration. But administrators remain an important part of the life of a classroom (and the evaluation of a teacher). Hence, the ideal solution for creating a learning environment at every level would likely require the involvement of administration.

PRINCIPAL LEADERSHIP

To this point, the focus of *Angels and Superheroes* has been on teachers. In classrooms, individual students' lives, the school, and the community, teachers have a crucial role to play in keeping schools focused on growing individuals rather than growing test scores. Nonetheless, since modeling change behavior is the catalyst for change, the role of the principal cannot be discounted.

Principals, like all leaders, are not superhuman, and they cannot be relied on or even asked to be the superheroes to the teachers' angels. Principals are humans, too. Principals must resist their own immunity to change. They must develop conversational capacity.

In *The Innovator's Mindset*, a powerful book about leading innovation and change in schools, George Couros states this idea powerfully: "I felt that, to lead a culture of innovation, it was crucial for me to be connected to the work that teachers were doing. My thought was: If my decisions had an impact on classrooms, then I wanted to immerse myself in the learning environments that inform those decisions."[8] He also describes the changes he made to align his actions as principal with his belief.

It is obvious that a principal is the person most influential in determining a culture in a school. This is not the work of one person, but one person can shape the work dramatically or prevent it from happening at all.

One principal, in presenting the coteaching used at his school at a workshop, allocated a portion of his time to sit with small groups of teachers and provide them a rationale for coteaching they could take back to their own principals. He knew they would have to advocate for themselves, because coteaching requires additional resources in a school, and principals must keep a careful eye on these resources. Giving them the capacity to make the argument from an administrator's viewpoint increased the chance they would be able to implement what they learned when they returned to their own schools.

Short of getting the administration fully behind an individual improvement or innovation in a school, the most powerful thing a principal can do is to get the administration out of the way. By removing obstacles and roadblocks, teachers can focus on their primary goals, creating an environment where learning can flourish.

By far the most invasive way an administrator can get involved in the classroom is through the teacher evaluation. At the beginning of this chapter, a teacher complained of her principal's open hostility toward different ideas and felt he was threatened by her expertise. It must be quite stressful to feel this way about your evaluator. Few people perform their best when their evaluator is present. This performance must only worsen when you feel your evaluator walks in with a negative view of your work.

One way principals can address this is to embrace the professional dialogue evaluation systems can help create. A full evaluation cycle should start with looking at key data and discussing strengths and weaknesses from both the teacher and administrator's perspective. From this discussion should arise one or more goals, which should be examined through the lens of the evaluation model used in the district or state, as applicable.

A common model used for teacher evaluation and improvement nationally is the Marzano framework. This structure includes conversation, a discussion of data, goal-setting, desired teacher actions and work, and a description of the support available from administration to create desired outcomes.

Although these frameworks are sometimes seen as rigid or even stultifying, there really is a great deal of flexibility in the language of the rubrics and frameworks. Teachers who are proactive in trying new approaches and conversant in the data regarding learning in their classrooms should find principals supportive of their efforts to innovate.

In these models, perhaps the most important component, and one easily overlooked in the urgency of the end of the year, is the final conference. A teacher deserves to know and hear directly from her administrator how her work matches up with the goals set at the start of the year in alignment with the objectives desired by the school and district. In this conference, a principal can clarify strengths and weaknesses, offer support and encouragement, and provide suggestions and resources in areas of needed improvement. It is easier to skip these conferences. It is better to structure and schedule them as a priority.

In reality, teaching is practically unquantifiable. Did teaching happen? Did a child learn? Was it because of what the teacher did? Did the teacher promote the learning or slow it down? Teaching is science and art. Perhaps another way for principals to help is to take the evaluative piece off the table altogether.

One principal had sought wisdom and growth everywhere she could imagine. She attended development for business managers, curriculum managers, teachers, and even data managers. She was constantly reading business bestsellers and teaching blogs. She knew one cannot anticipate where the next good idea will be discovered.

At separate trainings in 2010, one of which was the Cincinnati Public Schools ASCEND Institute, she encountered Rosamund and Benjamin Zander's provocative book *The Art of Possibility: Transforming Professional and Personal Life.*[9] In it, renowned conductor and teacher Ben Zanders relates advice on getting the best performance from the musicians in his care on stage and in his classroom.

One chapter gives details on transforming evaluation at the principal's school for two years, during which time the principal gave every teacher an A. The philosophy of "giving an 'A'" jibes with the core belief that all children want to learn. Teachers and administrators want to be successful at their work and be their best selves both at work and at home. Sometimes obstacles, for instance, the hidden immunity to change, prevent individuals from reaching their full potential. To undermine the voices that tell teachers, "Be just good enough to get by," "Try not to work too hard," "The contract says you do not have to do this," or "If you try that the principal will be upset," this administrator followed the advice from *The Art of Possibility*. She completely eliminated the evaluation. Actually, she went one step further by promising at the start of the year to give teachers the highest score on the evaluation at the end of the year.

At that time, her district's teacher evaluation had two parts: One was based on a school-selected goal, for example, addressing a specific state report card outcome; the other part was based on achieving a self-selected professional growth goal. It was for this second goal that she told her staff, in a letter, that she was giving them an "A."

> To take away evaluation anxiety as an impediment to teacher development and calculated risk-taking for the benefit of students, I am giving every teacher I evaluate this year the score of "exceeded" for their teacher-selected goal. The only catch (of course there is a catch, and it is a challenging one) is that you write me a letter that meets the following criteria:
>
> It must be written in the past tense, as if you wrote it in May 2012, looking back on this school year, starting with the sentence, "Dear Mrs. Seaver, I got my 'exceeded' rating because . . ."; it cannot include such phrases as "I will . . ." or "I intend to . . ."—this is you looking back on this year.
>
> It must explain why you earned the "exceeded" rating for your goal and describe not only specific goals met or work completed, but also the person you have become based on your effort to meet that goal this year. It is okay to be impressed with that person and the hard work and growth that was demonstrated.
>
> You must turn the letter in to me on or before your annual or PRE initial conferences.

She was not sure she was allowed to do this. She promised her staff she would give them the highest rating on half of their evaluation for writing a letter about what they hoped to achieve and who they hoped to become. That was *not* the intention of the teacher evaluation system.

Or was it? Didn't the district want to unleash their highly trained staff to be the best they could be? Anticipating an angry confrontation with the superintendent if this was ever discovered, she prepared her best defense and kept a copy on her phone so it would be present even if she had to defend herself without warning.

Ultimately, she never had to use it, but she was prepared, and it was short. "I learned it at the mandatory training. I assume you wanted me to *apply* what I learned there?" Her strongest defense would come later in the second year of implementing this practice.

The immediate reactions from teachers were strong. In preconferences with her, more than one teacher cried and expressed gratitude at feeling so supported. She suspected that some of them had never been asked by a leader to imagine the teacher they could become if they gave it everything they had. Some of them perhaps had never asked themselves that question at all.

The principal had just established an exceptionally high bar for administrative support for teaching. She had taken away the evaluation barrier that makes some teachers so nervous and causes some to second-guess themselves and take fewer instructional risks.

And she followed through. At the end of the year, it was rather simple to enter the scores for teachers who had written the letters. This was at the heart of her fear she might hear from the superintendent. It could look, on one hand, like she was simply dodging an onerous and time-consuming aspect of administration. She imagined the argument: "What if all the other principals simply announced they were giving an A?"

So, she gave this opportunity to her teachers. She received and read the letters, and provided encouragement and feedback. Between that time and the end of the year, she saw inspired teachers. They were engaging students, providing inventive lessons, wrestling with data, differentiating in the classroom, and working closely with academic coaches to improve instruction.

And in the end, she saw a group of professionals who lived up to their visions of themselves. They worked harder than ever, accepted her support and advice, and made improvements to practices as the year went on. The difference in the school was palpable, but there was a difference elsewhere, too.

Her first year using this approach she saw her school's state report card score jump two categories, from "continuous improvement" to "effective." The following year, her school was rated "excellent."

She now had her response to the question about what might happen if other principals found out about what she had done at her school. They might unleash the creativity and talent of teachers throughout the district and reach unexpected academic heights.

TIPS OF THE TRADE

- Create support for new teachers by reaching out to them individually, creating a support group, or advocating for intentional development by administration with a program like Teacher:Teacher.
- Experiment with the PLC model on your teaching team, within your discipline, or within another group of like-minded professionals.
- Learn and grow individually by reading relevant books, articles, and blogs about areas of concern.
- Attend relevant professional development (PD) or, if forced to attend a specific PD, intentionally seek out ways to make the advice and insights useful. Every PD offers some of these.
- Research with a partner.
- Try voluntary piloting with a group of willing participants.
- "Manage up" in supporting your principal to create the appropriate supports for yourself or others in the school.
- Use the existing evaluation system to your advantage by leveraging the available time to have meaningful conversations about improving instruction and defining best outcomes for students.
- Continue to advocate for a "growth mindset" model of teacher improvement. Teachers should be allowed to try new things and make "mistakes," which, in education, really means trying new approaches to solving a problem.

Notes

CHAPTER 1

1. "Criteria," *National Center for Education Statistics*. Retrieved December 22, 2016, from https://nces.ed.gov/nationsreportcard/NDEHelp/WebHelp/criteria.htm.

2. Peter Adamson, *Measuring Child Poverty: New League Tables of Child Poverty in the World's Rich Countries, UNICEF Office of Research*, May 2012. Retrieved June 3, 2017, from https://www.unicef-irc.org/publications/pdf/rc10_eng.pdf.

3. U.S. Department of Education, *Highlights from PISA 2009: Performance of U.S. 15-Year-Old Students in Reading, Mathematics, and Science Literacy in an International Context, National Center for Education Statistics*, 2010. Retrieved December 20, 2016, from https://nces.ed.gov/pubs2011/2011004.pdf.

4. Paul Tough, "How Kids Learn Resilience," *Atlantic*, May 16, 2016. Retrieved December 22, 2016, from www.theatlantic.com/magazine/archive/2016/06/how-kids-really-succeed/480744/.

5. *Adverse Childhood Experiences and the Lifelong Consequences of Trauma, American Academy of Pediatrics*, 2014. Retrieved June 3, 2017, from www.aap.org/en-us/Documents/ttb_aces_consequences.pdf.

6. Tough, "How Kids Learn Resilience," 3

7. Valerie Strauss, "Five Reasons Standardized Testing Isn't Likely to Let Up," *Washington Post*, March 11, 2015. Retrieved June 3, 2017, from www

.washingtonpost.com/news/answer-sheet/wp/2015/03/11/five-reasons-standardized-testing-isnt-likely-to-let-up/?utm_term=.1fe650bd6120%29.

8. "AFT Report Shows the High Cost of Overtesting," *American Federation of Teachers*, July 23, 2013. Retrieved June 3, 2017, from www.aft.org/news/aft-report-shows-high-cost-overtesting

9. Quinn Mulholland, "The Case against Standardized Testing," *Harvard Political Review*, May 14, 2015. Retrieved June 3, 2017, from http://harvardpolitics.com/united-states/case-standardized-testing/.

10. Jaime Greene, "Soft Skills: Preparing Kids for Life after School," *Association for Middle Level Education*, February 2016. Retrieved June 4, 2017, from www.amle.org/BrowsebyTopic/WhatsNew/WNDet/TabId/270/ArtMID/888/ArticleID/585/Soft-Skills-Preparing-Kids-for-Life-After-School.aspx.

11. Cory Turner, "Teachers Are Stressed, and That Should Stress Us All," *NPREd: How Learning Happens*, December 30, 2016. Retrieved June 3, 2017, from http://www.npr.org/sections/ed/2016/12/30/505432203/teachers-are-stressed-and-that-should-stress-us-all.

12. Eric Westervelt, "Frustration. Burnout. Attrition. It's Time to Address the National Teacher Shortage," *NPREd: How Learning Happens*, September 15, 2016. Retrieved June 3, 2017, from www.npr.org/sections/ed/2016/09/15/493808213/frustration-burnout-attrition-its-time-to-address-the-national-teacher-shortage.

13. "The Testing Industry's Big Four," *Frontline*. Retrieved June 4, 2017, from www.pbs.org/wgbh/pages/frontline/shows/schools/testing/companies.html.

14. Patrick O'Donnell, "Ohio Will Pay $23.6 Million to AIR for Common Core Tests Next Year," *Plain Dealer*, July 2, 2015. Retrieved July 7, 2017, from www.cleveland.com/metro/index.ssf/2015/07/ohio_will_pay_236_million_to_air_for_common_core_tests_next_year.html.

15. Alyssa Figueroa, "Eight Things You Should Know about Corporations Like Pearson That Make Huge Profits from Standardized Tests," *Alternet*, August 6, 2013. Retrieved June 3, 2017, from www.alternet.org/education/corporations-profit-standardized-tests.

16. Valerie Strauss, "Leading Mathematician Debunks 'Value-Added,'" *Washington Post*, May 9, 2011. Retrieved June 3, 2017, from www.washingtonpost.com/blogs/answer-sheet/post/leading-mathematician-debunks-value-added/2011/05/08/AFb999UG_blog.html?utm_term=.93ea84cfd25d.

17. Tough, "How Kids Learn Resilience," 9.

CHAPTER 2

1. Eric Siegel, "The Real Problem with Charles Murray and 'the Bell Curve,'" *Scientific American*, April 12, 2017. Retrieved August 30, 2017, from https://blogs.scientificamerican.com/voices/the-real-problem-with-charles-murray-and-the-bell-curve/#.

2. Nancy Flanagan, "Grading as an Opportunity to Encourage Students," *Education Week*, February 5, 2014. Retrieved August 30, 2017, from http://blogs.edweek.org/teachers/teacher_in_a_strange_land/2014/02/grading_as_an_opportunity_to_encourage_students.html?_ga=1.24700282.1541882594.1479433109.

3. "U.S. High School Graduation Rates," *Randy Sprick's Safe and Civil Schools*, reproduced from *Digest of Educational Statistics*, bulletin 1965, no. 4. Retrieved August 30, 2017, from www.safeandcivilschools.com/research/graduation_rates.php; Kenneth A. Simon and W. Vance Grant, *Digest of Educational Statistics: 1969 Edition, U.S Department of Health, Education, and Welfare*, September 1969. Retrieved August 30, 2017, from http://files.eric.ed.gov/fulltext/ED035996.pdf.

4. "Eleven Facts about High School Dropout Rates," *DoSomething.org*, 2017. Retrieved September 1, 2017, from www.dosomething.org/us/facts/11-facts-about-high-school-dropout-rates.

5. Norman L. Webb, "Depth-of-Knowledge Levels for Four Content Areas," *Wisconsin Center for Education Research*, March 28, 2002. Retrieved September 1, 2017, from http://facstaff.wcer.wisc.edu/normw/All%20content%20areas%20%20DOK%20levels%2032802.pdf.

6. Gerald Aungst, "Using Webb's Depth of Knowledge to Increase Rigor," *Edutopia*, September 4, 2014. Retrieved September 1, 2017, from www.edutopia.org/blog/webbs-depth-knowledge-increase-rigor-gerald-aungst.

7. Mihaly Csikszentmihalyi, *Flow* (New York: Harper Perennial Modern Classics, 2008).

8. Doug Lemov, *Teach Like a Champion: 49 Techniques That Put Students on the Path to College* (San Francisco, CA: Jossey-Bass, 2010).

9. Alfie Kohn, "Grading: The Issue Is Not How but Why," *AlfieKohn.org*, October 1994. Retrieved September 1, 2017, from www.alfiekohn.org/article/grading/.

10. Rachel Beth Rosales, "The Effects of Standards-Based Grading on Student Performance in Algebra 2," *Western Kentucky University TopSCHOLAR*, December 2013. Retrieved September 1, 2017, from http://digitalcommons.wku.edu/diss/53.

CHAPTER 3

1. Katherine C. Monahan, Sabrina Oesterle, and David J. Hawkins, "Predictors and Consequences of School Connectedness: The Case for Prevention," *Prevention Researcher* 17, no. 3 (September 1, 2010): 3–6. Retrieved March 6, 2017, from www2.pitt.edu/~adlab/People%20pics%20and%20links/Publications%20page/Predictors%20and%20Consequences%20of%20School%20Connectedness.pdf.

2. Monahan, Oesterle, and Hawkins, "Predictors and Consequences of School Connectedness."

3. Eric Schaps, "Creating a School Community," *Educational Leadership* 60, no. 6 (March 2003): 31–33.

4. M. D. Resnick, et al., "Protecting Adolescents from Harm: Findings from the National Longitudinal Study on Adolescent Health," *JAMA: Journal of the American Medical Association* 278, no. 10 (1997), doi:10.1001/jama.278.10.823.

5. Monahan, Oesterle, and Hawkins, "Predictors and Consequences of School Connectedness"

6. Monahan, Oesterle, and Hawkins, "Predictors and Consequences of School Connectedness."

7. Bonnie Benard, "Fostering Resilience in Children" (Urbana, IL: ERIC, 1995). ED386327.

8. "Parental Involvement in Schools," *Child Trends*, 2017. Retrieved March 6, 2017, from www.childtrends.org/indicators/parental-involvement-in-schools/.

9. Bari Walsh, "The Science of Resilience," *Harvard Graduate School of Education*, March 23, 2015. Retrieved March 6, 2017, from www.gse.harvard.edu/news/uk/15/03/science-resilience.

10. Benard, "Fostering Resilience in Children."

CHAPTER 4

1. Daniel Goleman, *Emotional Intelligence: Why It Can Matter More Than IQ* (New York: Bantam, 1995).

2. U.S. Department of Education Office for Civil Rights, "Civil Rights Data Collection Data Snapshot: School Discipline," *Education Week*, March 2014.

Retrieved March 6, 2017, from http://blogs.edweek.org/edweek/rulesforengagement/CRDC%20School%20Discipline%20Snapshot.pdf.

3. Caria Amurao, "Fact Sheet: How Bad Is the School-to-Prison Pipeline?" *PBS*, March 28, 2013. Retrieved March 6, 2017, from www.pbs.org/wnet/tavissmiley/tsr/education-under-arrest/school-to-prison-pipeline-fact-sheet/.

4. David C. Berliner and Bruce J. Biddle, *The Manufactured Crisis: Myths, Fraud, and the Attack on America's Public Schools* (New York: Perseus, 1995).

5. Victoria Purcell-Gates, *Other People's Words: The Cycle of Low Literacy* (Cambridge, MA: Harvard University Press, 1997), 4.

CHAPTER 5

1. Steven Slavik and Jon Carlson, *Readings in the Theory of Individual Psychology* (New York: Routledge, 2016), 232.

2. Katherine Reynolds Lewis, "What If Everything You Knew about Disciplining Kids Was Wrong?" *Mother Jones*, July/August 2015. Retrieved March 6, 2017, from http://www.motherjones.com/politics/2015/07/schools-behavior-discipline-collaborative-proactive-solutions-ross-greene/.

CHAPTER 6

1. Gene V. Glass, "Grouping Students for Instruction," in Alex Molnar, ed., *School Reform Proposals: The Research Evidence*, 95–112. Greenwich, CT: Information Age Publishing, 2002.

2. Robert E. Slavin, "Synthesis of Research on Grouping in Elementary and Secondary Schools," *Educational Leadership* (September 1988): 68.

3. Glass, "Grouping Students for Instruction."

4. Adam Gamoran, "Synthesis of Research: Is Ability Grouping Equitable?" *Educational Leadership* (October 1992): 11–17.

5. Gamoran, "Synthesis of Research."

6. Jeannie Oakes, *Keeping Track: How Schools Structure Inequality* (New Haven, CT: Yale University Press, 2005), 40.

7. Marge Scherer, "On Savage Inequalities: A Conversation with Jonathan Kozol," *Educational Leadership* (December 1992): 8.

8. Glass, "Grouping Students for Instruction."

9. Sonali Kohli, "Modern-Day Segregation in Public Schools," *Atlantic*, November 18, 2014. Retrieved July 13, 2017, from www.theatlantic.com/education/archive/2014/11/modern-day-segregation-in-public-schools/382846/.

10. Carol Ann Tomlinson, "Differentiation Does, in Fact, Work," *Education Week*, February 8, 2017. Retrieved June 19, 2017, from www.edweek.org/ew/articles/2015/01/28/differentiation-does-in-fact-work.html.

CHAPTER 7

1. John Kasich, "Annual State of the State Address," *Cleveland.com*, February 24, 2015. Retrieved September 1, 2017, from www.cleveland.com/open/index.ssf/2015/02/read_gov_john_kasichs_state_of.html.

2. Lyndsey Layton, "U.S. Schools Are Too Focused on Standardized Tests, Poll Says," *Washington Post*, August 23, 2015. Retrieved September 1, 2017, from www.washingtonpost.com/local/education/us-schools-are-too-focused-on-standardized-tests-poll-finds/2015/08/22/4a954396-47b3-11e5-8e7d-9c033e6745d8_story.html?utm_term=.f968f1608e3a.

3. Kenneth A. Simon and W. Vance Grant, *Digest of Educational Statistics: 1965 Edition* (Washington, DC: U.S. Government Printing Office, 1965).

4. Johns Hopkins University's School of Education, "Civic Marshall Plan to Build a Grad Nation. 2015 Index. Where Does Ohio Stand," accessed September 1, 2017, http://new.every1graduates.org/wp-content/uploads/2015/05/Ohio_2015.pdf

5. "Gamble Montessori High School," *Wikipedia*, November 7, 2015. Retrieved September 1, 2017, from https://en.wikipedia.org/wiki/Gamble_Montessori_High_School.

6. Mihaly Csikszentmihalyi, *Flow* (New York: Harper Perennial Modern Classics, 2008).

7. Maria Montessori, *The Montessori Method: Scientific Pedagogy as Applied to Child Education in "the Children's Houses"* (New York: Frederick A. Stokes Company, 1912).

8. M. C. R. Harrington, "An Ethnographic Comparison of Real and Virtual Field Trips to Trillium Trail: The Salamander Find as a Salient Event," *Children, Youth, and Environments* 19, no. 1 (2009): 74–101.

9. D. A. Kolb, *Experiential Learning: Experience as the Source of Learning and Development* (Englewood Cliffs, NJ: Prentice Hall, 1984), 26.

10. Rafe Esquith, *Teach Like Your Hair's on Fire: The Methods and Madness inside Room 56* (New York: Viking, 2007).

CHAPTER 8

1. Cory Turner, "Teachers Are Stressed, and That Should Stress Us All," *NPREd: How Learning Happens*, December 30, 2016. Retrieved June 3, 2017, from www.npr.org/sections/ed/2016/12/30/505432203/teachers-are-stressed-and-that-should-stress-us-all.

2. Brian Wansink and Jeffrey Sobal, "Mindless Eating: The 200 Daily Food Decisions We Overlook," *Sage Journals* 39, no. 1 (2007). Retrieved September 1, 2017, from https://foodpsychology.cornell.edu/research/mindless-eating-200-daily-food-decisions-we-overlook.

3. Lucinda Gray and Soheyla Taie, *Public School Teacher Attrition and Mobility in the First Five Years: Results from the First through Fifth Waves of the 2007–08 Beginning Teacher Longitudinal Study* (Washington, DC: U.S. Department of Education, National Center for Education Statistics, 2015).

4. Jennifer Gonzalez, "What Teachers Really Think about Principals," *Cultofpedagogy.com*, January 8, 2014. Retrieved September 1, 2017, from www.cultofpedagogy.com/what-teachers-really-think-about-principals/.

5. Duane Inman and Leslie Marlow, "Teacher Retention: Why Do Beginning Teachers Remain in the Profession?" *Education* 124, no. 4 (Summer 2004): 605–14.

6. Robert Kegan and Lisa Laskow Lahey, *Immunity to Change: How to Overcome It and Unlock the Potential in Yourself and Your Organization* (Boston: Harvard Business Press, 2009), 87.

7. Craig Weber, *Conversational Capacity: The Secret to Building Successful Teams That Perform When the Pressure Is On* (New York: McGraw-Hill Education, 2013), 15.

8. George Couros, *The Innovator's Mindset: Empower Learning, Unleash Talent, and Lead a Culture of Creativity* (San Diego, CA: Dave Burgess Consulting, 2015), 84.

9. Rosamund Zander and Benjamin Zander, *The Art of Possibility: Transforming Professional and Personal Life* (New York: Penguin, 2002).

Bibliography

Adamson, Peter. *Measuring Child Poverty: New League Tables of Child Poverty in the World's Rich Countries. UNICEF Office of Research*, May 2012. Retrieved June 3, 2017, from https://www.unicef-irc.org/publications/pdf/rc10_eng.pdf.

Adverse Childhood Experiences and the Lifelong Consequences of Trauma. American Academy of Pediatrics, 2004. Retrieved June 3, 2017, from www.aap.org/en-us/Documents/ttb_aces_consequences.pdf.

"AFT Report Shows the High Cost of Overtesting." *American Federation of Teachers*, July 23, 2013. Retrieved June 3, 2017, from www.aft.org/news/aft-report-shows-high-cost-overtesting.

Amurao, Caria. "Fact Sheet: How Bad Is the School-to-Prison Pipeline?" *PBS*, March 28, 2013. Retrieved March 6, 2017, from www.pbs.org/wnet/tavissmiley/tsr/education-under-arrest/school-to-prison-pipeline-fact-sheet/.

Aungst, Gerald. "Using Webb's Depth of Knowledge to Increase Rigor." *Edutopia*, September 4, 2014. Retrieved September 1, 2017, from www.edutopia.org/blog/webbs-depth-knowledge-increase-rigor-gerald-aungst.

Benard, Bonnie. "Fostering Resilience in Children." Urbana, IL: ERIC, 1995. ED386327.

Berliner, David C., and Bruce J. Biddle. *The Manufactured Crisis: Myths, Fraud, and the Attack on America's Public Schools*. New York: Perseus, 1995.

Couros, George. *The Innovator's Mindset: Empower Learning, Unleash Talent, and Lead a Culture of Creativity.* San Diego, CA: Dave Burgess Consulting, 2015.

"Criteria." *National Center for Education Statistics.* Retrieved December 22, 2016, from https://nces.ed.gov/nationsreportcard/NDEHelp/WebHelp/criteria.htm.

Csikszentmihalyi, Mihaly. *Flow.* New York: Harper Perennial Modern Classics, 2008.

"Eleven Facts about High School Dropout Rates." *DoSomething.org*, 2017. Retrieved September 1, 2017, from www.dosomething.org/us/facts/11-facts-about-high-school-dropout-rates.

Esquith, Rafe. *Teach Like Your Hair's on Fire: The Methods and Madness inside Room 56.* New York: Viking, 2007.

Figueroa, Alyssa. "Eight Things You Should Know about Corporations Like Pearson That Make Huge Profits from Standardized Tests." *Alternet*, August 6, 2013. Retrieved June 3, 2017, from www.alternet.org/education/corporations-profit-standardized-tests.

Flanagan, Nancy. "Grading as an Opportunity to Encourage Students." *Education Week*, February 5, 2014. Retrieved August 30, 2017, from http://blogs.edweek.org/teachers/teacher_in_a_strange_land/2014/02/grading_as_an_opportunity_to_encourage_students.html?_ga=1.24700282.1541882594.1479433109.

"Gamble Montessori High School." *Wikipedia*, November 7, 2015. Retrieved September 1, 2017, from https://en.wikipedia.org/wiki/Gamble_Montessori_High_School.

Gamoran, Adam. "Synthesis of Research: Is Ability Grouping Equitable?" *Educational Leadership* (October 1992): 11–17.

Glass, Gene V. "Grouping Students for Instruction." In Alex Molnar, ed., *School Reform Proposals: The Research Evidence*, 95–112. Greenwich, CT: Information Age Publishing, 2002.

Goleman, Daniel. *Emotional Intelligence: Why It Can Matter More Than IQ.* New York: Bantam, 1995.

Gonzalez, Jennifer. "What Teachers Really Think about Principals," *Cultofpedagogy.com*, January 8, 2014. Retrieved September 1, 2017, from www.cultofpedagogy.com/what-teachers-really-think-about-principals/.

Gray, Lucinda, and Soheyla Taie. *Public School Teacher Attrition and Mobility in the First Five Years: Results from the First through Fifth Waves of the 2007–08 Beginning Teacher Longitudinal Study*. Washington, DC: U.S. Department of Education, National Center for Education Statistics, 2015.

Greene, Jaime. "Soft Skills: Preparing Kids for Life after School." *Association for Middle Level Education*, February 2016. Retrieved June 4, 2017, from www.amle.org/BrowsebyTopic/WhatsNew/WNDet/TabId/270/ArtMID/888/ArticleID/585/Soft-Skills-Preparing-Kids-for-Life-After-School.aspx.

Harrington, M. C. R. "An Ethnographic Comparison of Real and Virtual Field Trips to Trillium Trail: The Salamander Find as a Salient Event." *Children, Youth, and Environments* 19, no. 1 (2009): 74–101.

Inman, Duane, and Leslie Marlow. "Teacher Retention: Why Do Beginning Teachers Remain in the Profession?" *Education* 124, no. 4 (Summer 2004): 605–14.

Johns Hopkins University School of Education. *Civic Marshall Plan to Build a Grad Nation, 2015 Index: Where Does Ohio Stand, Everyone Graduates Center*, 2015. Retrieved September 1, 2017, from http://new.every1graduates.org/wp-content/uploads/2015/05/Ohio_2015.pdf.

Kasich, John. "Annual State of the State Address." *Cleveland.com*, February 24, 2015. Retrieved September 1, 2017, from www.cleveland.com/open/index.ssf/2015/02/read_gov_john_kasichs_state_of.html.

Kegan, Robert, and Lisa Laskow Lahey. *Immunity to Change: How to Overcome It and Unlock the Potential in Yourself and Your Organization*. Boston: Harvard Business Press, 2009.

Kohli, Sonali. "Modern-Day Segregation in Public Schools." *Atlantic*, November 18, 2014. Retrieved July 13, 2017, from www.theatlantic.com/education/archive/2014/11/modern-day-segregation-in-public-schools/382846/.

Kohn, Alfie. "Grading: The Issue Is Not How but Why." *AlfieKohn.org*, October 1994. Retrieved September 1, 2017, from www.alfiekohn.org/article/grading/.

Kolb, D. A. *Experiential Learning: Experience as the Source of Learning and Development*. Englewood Cliffs, NJ: Prentice Hall, 1984.

Layton, Lyndsey. "U.S. Schools Are Too Focused on Standardized Tests, Poll Says." *Washington Post*, August 23, 2015. Retrieved September 1, 2017, from www.

washingtonpost.com/local/education/us-schools-are-too-focused-on-standardized-tests-poll-finds/2015/08/22/4a954396-47b3-11e5-8e7d-9c033e6745d8_story.html?utm_term=.f968f1608e3a.

Lemov, Doug. *Teach Like a Champion: 49 Techniques That Put Students on the Path to College.* San Francisco, CA: Jossey-Bass, 2010.

Lewis, Katherine Reynolds. "What If Everything You Knew about Disciplining Kids Was Wrong?" *Mother Jones*, July/August 2015. Retrieved March 6, 2017, from http://www.motherjones.com/politics/2015/07/schools-behavior-discipline-collaborative-proactive-solutions-ross-greene/.

Monahan, Katherine C., Sabrina Oesterle, and David J. Hawkins. "Predictors and Consequences of School Connectedness: The Case for Prevention." *Prevention Researcher* 17, no. 3 (September 1, 2010): 3–6. Retrieved March 6, 2017, from www2.pitt.edu/~adlab/People%20pics%20and%20links/Publications%20page/Predictors%20and%20Consequences%20of%20School%20Connectedness.pdf.

Montessori, Maria. *The Montessori Method: Scientific Pedagogy as Applied to Child Education in "the Children's Houses."* New York: Frederick A. Stokes Company, 1912.

Mulholland, Quinn. "The Case against Standardized Testing." *Harvard Political Review*, May 14, 2015. Retrieved June 3, 2017, from http://harvardpolitics.com/united-states/case-standardized-testing/.

Nelson, Jane, and Lynn Lott. "Mistaken Goals Chart." *Positivediscipline.com.* Retrieved March 27, 2016, from www.positivediscipline.com/sites/default/files/mistakengoalchart.pdf.

Oakes, Jeannie. *Keeping Track: How Schools Structure Inequality.* New Haven, CT: Yale University Press, 2005.

O'Donnell, Patrick. "Ohio Will Pay $23.6 Million to AIR for Common Core Tests Next Year." *Plain Dealer*, July 2, 2015. Retrieved July 7, 2017, from www.cleveland.com/metro/index.ssf/2015/07/ohio_will_pay_236_million_to_air_for_common_core_tests_next_year.html.

"Parental Involvement in Schools." *Child Trends*, 2017. Retrieved March 6, 2017, from www.childtrends.org/indicators/parental-involvement-in-schools/.

Purcell-Gates, Victoria. *Other People's Words: The Cycle of Low Literacy.* Cambridge, MA: Harvard University Press, 1997.

Resnick, M. D., et al. "Protecting Adolescents from Harm: Findings from the National Longitudinal Study on Adolescent Health." *JAMA: Journal of the American Medical Association* 278, no. 10 (1997), doi:10.1001/jama.278.10.823.

Rosales, Rachel Beth. "The Effects of Standards-Based Grading on Student Performance in Algebra 2." *Western Kentucky University TopSCHOLAR*, December 2013. Retrieved September 1, 2017, from http://digitalcommons.wku .edu/diss/53.

Schaps, Eric. "Creating a School Community." *Educational Leadership* 60, no. 6 (March 2003): 31–33.

Scherer, Marge. "On Savage Inequalities: A Conversation with Jonathan Kozol." *Educational Leadership* (December 1992): 4–9.

Siegel, Eric. "The Real Problem with Charles Murray and 'the Bell Curve.'" *Scientific American*, April 12, 2017. Retrieved August 30, 2017, from https://blogs .scientificamerican.com/voices/the-real-problem-with-charles-murray-and-the -bell-curve/#.

Simon, Kenneth A., and W. Vance Grant. *Digest of Educational Statistics: 1965 Edition*. Washington, DC: U.S. Government Printing Office, 1965.

Simon, Kenneth A., and W. Vance Grant. *Digest of Educational Statistics: 1969 Edition. U.S Department of Health, Education, and Welfare*, September 1969. Retrieved August 30, 2017, from http://files.eric.ed.gov/fulltext/ED035996.pdf.

Slavik, Steven, and Jon Carlson. *Readings in the Theory of Individual Psychology*. New York: Routledge, 2016.

Slavin, Robert E. "Synthesis of Research on Grouping in Elementary and Secondary Schools." *Educational Leadership* (September 1988): 67–77.

Strauss, Valerie. "Five Reasons Standardized Testing Isn't Likely to Let Up." *Washington Post*, March 11, 2015. Retrieved June 3, 2017, from www .washingtonpost.com/news/answer-sheet/wp/2015/03/11/five-reasons -standardized-testing-isnt-likely-to-let-up/?utm_term=.1fe650bd6120%29.

Strauss, Valerie. "Leading Mathematician Debunks 'Value-Added.'" *Washington Post*, May 9, 2011. Retrieved June 3, 2017, from www.washingtonpost.com/blogs/ answer-sheet/post/leading-mathematician-debunks-value-added/2011/05/08/ AFb999UG_blog.html?utm_term=.93ea84cfd25d.

"The Testing Industry's Big Four." *Frontline.* Retrieved June 4, 2017, from http://www.pbs.org/wgbh/pages/frontline/shows/schools/testing/companies.html.

Tomlinson, Carol Ann. "Differentiation Does, in Fact, Work." *Education Week*, February 8, 2017. Retrieved June 19, 2017, from www.edweek.org/ew/articles/2015/01/28/differentiation-does-in-fact-work.html.

Tough, Paul. "How Kids Learn Resilience." *Atlantic*, May 16, 2016. Retrieved December 22, 2016, from www.theatlantic.com/magazine/archive/2016/06/how-kids-really-succeed/480744/.

Turner, Cory. "Teachers Are Stressed, and That Should Stress Us All." *NPREd: How Learning Happens*, December 30, 2016. Retrieved June 3, 2017, from http://www.npr.org/sections/ed/2016/12/30/505432203/teachers-are-stressed-and-that-should-stress-us-all.

U.S. Department of Education. *Highlights from PISA 2009: Performance of U.S. 15-Year-Old Students in Reading, Mathematics, and Science Literacy in an International Context. National Center for Education Statistics*, 2010. Retrieved December 20, 2016, from https://nces.ed.gov/pubs2011/2011004.pdf.

U.S. Department of Education Office for Civil Rights. "Civil Rights Data Collection Data Snapshot: School Discipline." *Education Week*, March 2014. Retrieved March 6, 2017, from http://blogs.edweek.org/edweek/rulesforengagement/CRDC%20School%20Discipline%20Snapshot.pdf.

"U.S. High School Graduation Rates." *Randy Sprick's Safe and Civil Schools*, reproduced from *Digest of Educational Statistics*, bulletin 1965, no. 4. Retrieved August 30, 2017, www.safeandcivilschools.com/research/graduation_rates.php.

Walsh, Bari. "The Science of Resilience." *Harvard Graduate School of Education*, March 23, 2015. Retrieved March 6, 2017, from www.gse.harvard.edu/news/uk/15/03/science-resilience.

Wansink, Brian, and Jeffrey Sobal. "Mindless Eating: The 200 Daily Food Decisions We Overlook." *Sage Journals* 39, no. 1 (2007). Retrieved September 1, 2017, from https://foodpsychology.cornell.edu/research/mindless-eating-200-daily-food-decisions-we-overlook.

Webb, Norman L. "Depth-of-Knowledge Levels for Four Content Areas." *Wisconsin Center for Education Research*, March 28, 2002. Retrieved September 1, 2017, from http://facstaff.wcer.wisc.edu/normw/All%20content%20areas%20%20DOK%20levels%2032802.pdf.

Weber, Craig. *Conversational Capacity: The Secret to Building Successful Teams That Perform When the Pressure Is On*. New York: McGraw-Hill Education, 2013.

Westervelt, Eric. "Frustration. Burnout. Attrition. It's Time to Address the National Teacher Shortage." *NPREd: How Learning Happens*, September 15, 2016. Retrieved June 3, 2017, from www.npr.org/sections/ed/2016/09/15/493808213/frustration-burnout-attrition-its-time-to-address-the-national-teacher-shortage.

Zander, Rosamund, and Benjamin Zander. *The Art of Possibility: Transforming Professional and Personal Life*. New York: Penguin, 2002.

About the Authors

Jack M. Jose is principal of Gamble Montessori High School, a Cincinnati Public School (CPS) serving grades seven through 12. He has held this position for nine years, having taught English at the same school for one year prior. Before that he was an English teacher and Paideia Program facilitator at Hughes Center, a CPS school, for 13 years.

Jose's education includes administrative licensure from Xavier University in Cincinnati, Ohio; a master's degree in curriculum and instruction from the University of Cincinnati; and a bachelor of arts degree in English education from Miami University in Oxford, Ohio. He also has a Montessori secondary I and II credential through the Cincinnati Montessori Secondary Teacher Education Program. He earned National Board Certification in early adolescent English language arts in 1997.

Jose has participated in the ASCEND Leadership Training Institute, the Ohio State Executive Leadership Academy, and Harvard University's "Improving Schools: The Art of Leadership" urban principals program.

During the year this book was being written, Jose completed his first half-marathon and recorded an album of original songs (available on your favorite streaming service). What little free time he has, he enjoys with his wife and their two young adult children.

Krista L. Taylor has been an intervention specialist at Gamble Montessori High School for eight years. She earned her M.S. in education through Wheelock College in Boston, Massachusetts, and her B.A. in history from Kenyon College in Gambier, Ohio. Additionally, she holds an AMS Montessori secondary I and II credential through CMStep, a secondary Montessori teacher education program in Cincinnati.

Taylor's work experience has spanned a wide variety of service delivery models, including instruction using pull-out intervention, teaching a self-contained SBH/ED classroom, providing inclusion intervention, and developing and implementing coteaching practices to support inclusion. She has also served as special education team leader and interdisciplinary junior high team leader. Moreover, she works as an instructor and field consultant for aspiring Montessori teachers at CMStep.

In 2015, Taylor was selected to be the Western and Southern Lawrence C. Hawkins Educator of the Year in Cincinnati Public Schools. In her speech, she noted that "none of us are angels or superheroes," and thousands of teachers deserve the award each year. That summer, the Cincinnati City Council celebrated "Krista L. Taylor Day" in Cincinnati to honor her decision to provide the entire amount of her $10,000 cash award to the Gamble Montessori Foundation, stipulating that it be used as scholarships for students who provide leadership by looking out for other students.

What little free time she has, she enjoys with her husband and their two children. And on occasion, she finds time to sit on a rock in the middle of a creek in the woods and read a good book.

Taylor's "Educator of the Year" speech gave their cult-favorite blog, AngelsAndSuperheroes.com, its tongue-in-cheek name. Through the weekly blog and this book, they hope to share best practices for helping every teacher remember that as educators, children's spirits, and not their test scores, should remain our primary focus.